MW00674649

BYE BYE BAGS

LAUGHING TO LIGHTEN YOUR LOAD!

THE KIANA DANCIE

3D Media Ent. Group

Library of Congress Control Number: 2021920545
ISBN 978-0-57830330-6-9
Printed in the United States of America

This book is a recount of the author's present recollections of experiences over time. Some names and characteristics have been changed, some events have been compressed, and some dialogue has been recreated.

DEDICATION

There is no dance without the Dancies.

"He will once again fill your mouth with laughter and your lips with shouts of joy."
- Job 8:21

"You can make the future, but it starts with leaving the past..."

-Immortal Technique

TABLE OF CONTENTS

Baggage: *Past experiences or long-held ideas regarded as burdens and impediments. Its general concern is with unresolved issues of an emotional nature, often with an implication that the emotional baggage is detrimental.*

ABOUT THE AUTHOR

Having always been the life of the party with a dynamic personality and a glowing smile, The Kiana Dancie is a powerhouse comedian, transformational speaker, media personality, actress & entrepreneur on and off stage. She has shared several dynamic and colorful life experiences on her sold-out comedy tour "Single in the City" across the country. Kiana was one of the original hosts of the TV One nationally syndicated talk show "Sister Circle Live" and destroyed the stage on the TV ONE hit show "Whose Got Jokes?" with host Bill Bellamy. She was also introduced as a beast by host Rodney Perry of the Bounce show "Off the Chain." Her amazing set during the filming of Kevin Hart's LOL at the 2018 Montreal Comedy Festival led to her casting in two movies – a BET & Showtime feature "One CrazyChristmas" and the Marlon Wayans

Netflix hit "Sextuplets." Kiana has toured with Dave Chappelle, Kountry Wayne, Jess Hilarious, Earthquake, and many more. As a proud mama's girl and big sister, she enjoys spending time with her family. In addition to blazing stages, she is also the owner of the Duluth, GA location of the franchise CPR Cell Phone Repair and a 2022 recipient of The President's Lifetime Achievement Award for her commitment to building stronger communities through volunteering.

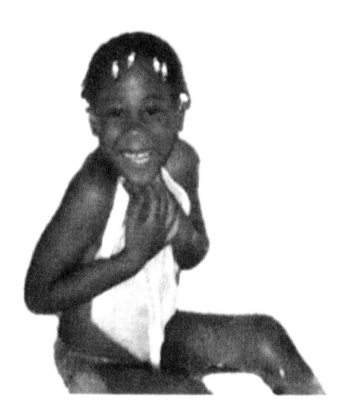

clean
Happy^me...

INTRODUCTION

After another attempted move to L.A., I got cast to appear on Lifetime's new reality show, Atlanta Plastic, following three Black plastic surgeons in Atlanta, Georgia. As I spoke with the casting director, I wondered if I really wanted to be on national TV. How good are these doctors? Do they really know what they're doing? Lord, I don't know if I want them working on me. Having researched the show, it turned out to be a great opportunity to gain additional exposure as both a stand-up comedian and actress. It was also an amazing opportunity to get the cosmetic work I wanted. My appearance on Atlanta Plastic served as more than a way for millions to see my signature red lips and pretty gapped teeth smile. It was finally an opportunity to get the bags under my eyes removed.

No one likes to look in the mirror and see bags under their eyes, but almost everyone over the age of twenty-five is familiar with this experience. As you get older, they become more common, staring back at you when you look at yourself in the morning. The bags made me look tired, old, and, yes, tired! LOL

People were always asking, "Are you sleepy? You okay, girl? Are you resting?" All I could say was, "Yes, I'm getting rest. It's these damn bags under my eyes, which I've always had! Courtesy of my father." Honey, if he was gonna give me bags, he could have at least made them designer! There's nothing wrong with a little Chanel or Hermés sitting in the front seat of my Beemer. As disgusted as I was about these genetic marks of distinction, I never had the time or money to spare to get the procedure done.

My bags were a huge frustration for me. I have spent many hours trying to conceal them.

People never saw what I thought was a major flaw as a problem. Instead, people wanted to talk to me about the gap in my teeth. I felt no kind of way about the gap in my teeth because my mom has one, and most of the women in my family have or had one. So, if you don't have a gap, we all question whether you're really a Dancie.

My bags were an unwanted, highly undesirable, heavy gift from my father, who also carried the burden of his life's struggles under his eyes. I can remember thinking to myself that these bags will never be cute. Ever! Not today or tomorrow. It frustrated me so much! People would swear that I was not sleeping well, or I should stop whatever I was doing to make them bigger. Like I would really sit at home and try to grow bags on my face! For what? To prove that I was...Um, crazy?! LOL! Whatever! While this all irritated me greatly, I had to bring myself to the conclusion that I would have to do something about them.

I needed to deal with this issue immediately. I started with the definition. Bags are anything you can carry, store things in, or remove things from.

Bags can consist of experiences, memories, things you wanted, and things you didn't. Things that people gave or things left with you. Bags can be people, places, experiences, memories, or things you can learn from and teach others. They can be heavy or light, nice or mean. But at the end of the day, you don't have to carry them.

That's how I felt about my under-eye baggage. Even though I've had these bags for my entire life, and they have never given me problems, they were still something I wanted to get rid of. I knew that the surgery was necessary, especially being in this highly judgmental industry they call show business!

I finally realized that I didn't have to carry these unsightly bags under my eyes any more than I needed to carry the weight of the fear of failure, insecurities, being a child molestation survivor, and the failed relationships in my life. My decision to remove the physical bags from my face resulted in the subliminal removal of the emotional bags I carried in my spirit. It was time to let go and move forward with God's plan for my life, and it couldn't be done lugging pieces of the past around.

Perhaps the bags underneath our eyes were the body's way of telling us we carry too much in our hearts.

Bye, Bye, Bags was written to share the story of how removing the bags from my eyes allowed me to remove the emotional scars I'd been very open about yet unwilling to discard. The title of this book speaks of all the things that were going on in my life, the emotions I dealt with, and the baggage I had accumulated.

Although I carried extra baggage, I never allowed them to define me. However, they will give you a little insight into who I am and what I've been through. From them, you will understand that even in the face of weakness, there's never a day that giving up is or has been an option. My past does not have to dictate my future. I'm a survivor and so are you.

When you're going through trials, you have to learn to laugh. I often tell people even if you're not sure what you're laughing about, the energy it takes to laugh will release a chemical inside of your body that will give you the power to heal. Sometimes in the midst of crying, you must allow yourself to laugh, crying is cleansing to the soul, but laughter uplifts your heart. Sometimes, a good laugh and a good "Komedy Kocktail" are all you need to get through your day. I've come to understand that people come to my shows to laugh and forget about all the mess they're going through.

I enjoy being able to use my gift to make people laugh and give them the opportunity to release and not stress about what they are going through. We all need that. A long time ago, I made myself a promise that I would not allow my bags to get so heavy that I couldn't carry them. I would not let them get so full that I could not even remember what I was carrying, i.e., what I was crying, mad, bothered, or sad about anymore. No matter what I'm going through, I will stop, reflect, and laugh at my problems. Then I'll figure out a solution to my issues.

Once I've kept that promise, I've concluded that my issues are not so bad, they're not so heavy, and they're not stronger than I am. They may be paper, garbage, or plastic bags, but they'll never defeat me, nor should yours defeat you.

We have the choice to pick those bags up and continue to carry them or the power to unpack them and let them go.

This is a decision that anyone can make, even if you're in the middle of your mess. Regardless of where you find yourself in your issue, you can choose whether you'll carry that emotional baggage around with you or release it. We can either harbor emotions from our past or unlock our futures. The choice is ours to make.

Getting rid of the bags under my eyes was a TRUE eye-opener! HA! It was essentially a reminder of my life trauma and my life drama. While healing from this procedure, I was given time to think, reflect, and yes... Laugh! This helped me to see how much emotional baggage I held onto in my life. I can't say if I ignored it or not, but I know it's something that I hadn't dealt with efficiently.

My lack of dealing was a choice, a decision, and, in hindsight, it was not the best decision. I wrote this book so you can make the decisions that will help you laugh through your baggage. You have a choice. You can unpack those bags, pick them up, carry them around, or let them go.

Lately, I've been in a 'set them on fire' frame of mind! No need to keep them around if they're reminders of old wounds and bad days. You have total control over what each day will be like. Will it be a good day or not? It's all up to you! You can decide if you want to carry them or not. You can drop them at the front door and never pick them up again, or you can throw them over a damn bridge.

At the end of the day, do something more than let them weigh you down. As you read the pages of this book, I hope you will make a conscious decision to recognize your baggage, choose to be happy, and say bye, bye bags! I'm laughing to lighten my load!

66 *The best way to treat obstacles is to use them as stepping stones. Laugh at them, tread on them, and let them lead you to something better.* **99**

Enid Blyton

> **"** *The world can't tell you who you are. You've just got to figure out who you are and there, for better or worse.* **"**
>
> **Dave Chappelle**

One

COMING TO THE STAGE

As loud as people think I am, believe it or not, I'm actually quiet. It's one of those situations where I am paid to be loud and perform jokes. However, when I am at home, sometimes I say nothing.

My mother always says, "You're so creepy, you don't talk," and every time she does, I laugh. I find it interesting that people assume I am "on" all the time and that it's always going to be showtime when they're around me. Not so! People don't realize that I possess many complicated layers which come together to make the one and only "The Kiana Dancie." To love me is to understand the expression,

11

"It is what it is." I enjoy the mysterious part of myself.

Most people don't know who I am or what I've been through. Those who see me on stage or on television think my life is glamorous and amazing as if I have no worries or troubles. Although my life is filled with amazing things, I have been through some STUFF!

I've learned to perfect the art of "Everything is amazing!" You see, I'm solid and well put together when you look at me. I'm smiling, showing my dazzling white teeth amid my big red lips, looking like I don't have a care in the world. Of course, I am all the 'wells,' well dressed, well-educated, and yes, even well-traveled. But most people don't know the baggage I carry, and that's okay because my bags don't define who I am. More than anything, my baggage might give you a little insight into Kiana's world.

If you decide to keep reading this book, you will learn enough about me to go, 'Oh my God, I didn't know she was molested,' or 'Oh my God, I didn't know she fears retaliation from her boyfriend's killer! She seems to have it all together.' I do have it together, but I'm human too. To be honest, I'm not that deep. I am what you see, a woman on a mission laser-focused on winning.

We all carry baggage from our past or current situations, and I am no different. My saving grace was my mother, who had enough sense to send me to someone to talk to when I was going through my trials, and she never ever stopped praying for and over me.

Learning how to process, carry, and control my bags were valuable lessons. So much so that I was never disturbed in my spirit by the things that had happened to me. Now, there may have been situations where I was accused of being too feisty, assertive, or aggressive. I've even been called cold or an eccedentesiast, (i.e., a person who hides their pain behind a smile). This may have been a derivative of transporting my baggage, never seeing myself as damaged. I did not deny having baggage and took the time to acknowledge the load. However, once I embraced my bags, they became easier to manage and continue to carry.

I can't undo what I've been through, nor do I have any shame in my stories – as you will see as you read on. The beautiful thing about my life is just that – it's beautiful! I am the co-author of my life, so when I tell you something about me, trust me, it's the way I wanted you to know it, and in case you decide to retell my story, I want to be sure you have the TRUTH! ALL FACTS ABOUT ME!

When you hear my story, I want you to learn from it, pick something up, and apply it to your life. Yes, I went through some things and based on that, I may be able to help you. I'm not ashamed. I haven't done anything wrong, and if I did do something wrong, I'd own that too!

I'm comfortable in my own skin despite any challenges and what you may think about me after hearing my stories. I don't understand how people aren't comfortable in their own skin. If you're feeling this way, I want you to remember this: It's YOUR SKIN! No one is you – and that is your superpower! In fact, you should be uncomfortable in somebody else's skin. Trying to be like them, live like them, shoot, trying to *be* them! LOL!

See over the years, I've learned that people are going to judge you. You can assume that when you're walking down the street, somebody is going to have their own perception of you. Learn not to give a damn! In fact, I've always been the one that could care less about what anyone thought of me, especially if they didn't take the time to figure me out. That has always been the tune I moved to and the attitude I've carried.

As a child, my mother would tell me, "What other people think about you will never matter. You are the only one that should feel some type of way if you don't like you." My experiences have shaped me into a person who understands what a gift it is to let go and let God, embracing every situation that has impacted my life. Without His mercy, I am nothing.

As much fussing and cussing as I do, best believe I know who keeps me whole and covered. I'm a child of God, whether I've gotten drunk all night or had a one-night stand (not saying that I ever have LOL)! Despite my faults, I get on my knees and talk to God. I confess, "I'm not perfect. I didn't mean to do that, help me." It doesn't matter, I'm going to pray for forgiveness, honey! I always pray, "Lord, if I take one step toward You, please take two steps toward me because I'm not strong enough. I'm not perfect, and I love you!"

I've called on the name of Jesus many times to help me cope with situations in my life. If I wasn't calling on the Lord, I was calling my mamma. My mother means the world to me. I'll always have her back and she'll always have mine. I know I was a bit much to handle as a young child and Lord knows as a teenager, she probably wanted to kill me many times, but she loved me and never gave up on me.

You'll have to ask my mother what kind of child I was when I was growing up. In my view, I was wild! Definitely crazy and always in something! I remember I used to steal my mom's car with no license and drive it to my play brother's house so he could drive it because he had his license! LOL! At least I was responsible with my mischief! Now, isn't that crazy?

Although smoking, drinking, and doing drugs weren't my thing, mostly because I was too scared, it's a blessing that I'm even here. I'm sure I gave my mother plenty of heart attacks behaving like a crazy person! I was a boy-crazy, sassy teenager. I've always been a little too grown. I was a little lady, playing in dress shoes and not sneakers like most kids. I would walk around with a purse and white gloves and introduce myself to complete strangers as "The Kiana Dancie." I wanted to do my hair, wear lip gloss, and dress like I was going to the coronation. It was way too much. I wore a dress every day going to Catholic school, so I always looked polished.

My mother played her part in making sure I always looked nice. To this day, I don't like sneakers. I think life made me this way because I was always around a lot of grown people. Being the only child from my mother, who is the baby of five sisters, most of their kids were older than me so I always hung out with my older cousins. I gained a lot of experience in how to carry myself in a certain way from playing with them.

My older family members gave me an opportunity to act like I was grown, just like they did with my mother when she was young. My mom grew up quickly because she was on her own to a certain extent. My mother's mother died when my mom was nine years old which caused my mom to grow up fast. Although my grandfather was there to raise my mom and her five sisters, he didn't know what to do after becoming an instant single father of six daughters!

My grandfather worked for GMC for thirty years and never, ever missed a day of work. He did his best, despite being a functional alcoholic and later being diagnosed with Alzheimer's disease. My mother was always a little lady. So, when she was pushed to grow up quickly, it came naturally to her.

Nobody F**** with My Click

My mother and I have a bond that's extraordinary and unbreakable. Most girls relish the idea of being called a "daddy's girl." I am the complete opposite. I am a mama's girl! I am NOT ASHAMED of it either! Maybe that's why I've always felt obligated to help my mom. She has been my biggest supporter, ALWAYS. My family and I are a solid unit. If one has, then we all have. I can recall a time when I lied on my job application to get my first job. I said I was fourteen years old, but I had just turned thirteen. When I started working, I gave my whole paycheck to my mother. I wanted to help my mom and repay her for everything she had done for me.

The day my mother had my little brother, it was as if I had had my own child. I always say I'm a childless mother. I did everything for that boy but give birth to him. There was never a day that I was not in love with him, which is kind of ironic.

At first, the idea of having a little brother was disgusting because I was the only child forever. I gained great enjoyment in being the only child of my mother. I enjoyed shopping with my mom and not having to share my things or my mother. It was just me and her! Me and my mommy! I can remember the day that she told me she was pregnant. It was like I was telling her I was pregnant! I felt so much disappointment. I couldn't explain it. I cried. I was mad and I was angry. But the day my mother had my brother, changed me.

I fell in love with him. His hands and feet were so small, his eyes were so big, and his skin was so soft. It softened my heart and made me understand that I needed to set a certain example. That was the day I decided that he wouldn't want for anything. He was my little brother and I, as his big sister, would always strive to make him proud. I would always support him, and he would never have a bigger fan than me!

When I am on stage, I talk about my brother sometimes. He's definitely part of my set. He's given me so much inspiration and keeps me reaching higher. I don't think Eric, my brother, minds anymore. He's not impressed with much. LOL! If you know the Dancies, you'll know that we're not impressed by anything. He knows I'm being honest, and this is what I do. I tell jokes and I tell the truth about my reality. He would say, 'That's just Yana," calling me by my nickname. In his mind, I'm simply doing me. He's quiet, calculated, and easygoing, and I am the loud one! I am the one that people can't miss in the room, usually because I'm telling you, "I am The Kiana Dancie and you should know me!"

Ironically, sometimes my brother will say something, and I'll think, 'Wait a minute, this dude is kind of profound,' and I'll wonder where that came from. He doesn't talk much, but when he does, you better stop and listen because it's going to be good, kind of like our mom.

By the time my brother was born, I was already carrying bags of emotional scars. I never thought about exposing my bags to my brother, but if he were going through something, maybe my life could help. My bags would prove that life is hard, things are tough, and you can't always predict what is going to happen. You don't know what your life is going to be like today or tomorrow, but if you keep living, life will get better. Like the tide of the sea, things will change, and when you let go of those bags of emotions, that will be the day your life will become easier. Despite what you may have been told, being happy is your right, but it's also always your choice. You have to decide how you want your life to go and how much baggage you want to take with you.

21

My mother always told me the path that people take in life is not all our own decision. It belongs to God first, but we do have control of the process. We can decide how easy we'll make that process. What keeps us from going in that direction is fear of the past, our baggage. I laugh at life sometimes because I believe the devil is always busy trying to stop the flow of my blessings, and if I had allowed it, he would have won.

It's human to be afraid. It's our initial response. If you see something you don't understand, or you run into something you're not clear about, then it's only natural for a person to respond by being afraid. For me, I had to remember I'm cut from a different cloth. I'm a child of God; I'm His favorite, and always have been. I can't allow my baggage to stop me. I had to speak to my bags and say, 'Get out of my way, honey! I have things to do and it's not carrying you around.' In my heart, I may be scared, but I can't let the devil know that I'm scared. I can't show any signs of fear. I had to learn how to give my worries to God. That's why I'm laughing.

I'm laughing at the devil saying, 'Nothing you do could ever stop me or slow me down!'

Let's be clear, if and/or when you decide to get rid of your baggage, the enemy is going to take that personally! He will start throwing all kinds of stuff in your direction. This is the time that you must arm yourself with prayer and get rid of those around you that don't believe in you and your dreams. Get rid of those that don't speak life into your vision. Pray for clarity. Pray for serenity. And most importantly, pray for strength to stay the course because when you're chasing a dream, it won't be easy.

I always tell myself I am who I am. So, I carry no shame or guilt about my past. I'm not living my life for anybody else's pleasure, or for anybody else's approval. Every day I wake up and say, "I am a Dancie and I will conduct myself as such!"

I will never allow myself to give up. I never use the words can't and won't. Instead, I use the phrases you will, you can, and you should. Using these words of affirmation to deal with my bags and even my dreams, make me feel like nothing is impossible for me.

Since you've picked up this book, I want you to make a conscious decision to do the same. I'm being very transparent. When you see me on stage with the glitz and the glamour being funny, you don't know my struggles. You don't know that money gets tight. You don't know that I am a child molestation survivor. You would never know that I have had trust issues with both men and women! On a normal day you see me laughing, but don't know I'm crying inside. You have no idea. The only thing you know is that you bought a ticket to a comedy show and want to be entertained, and that's what I need to bring to the stage... ENTERTAINMENT!

I'm New, But Not Brand New

Many people think that I'm 'brand new' now because I've had a little success. But I have always been this person. I have been both sides of the coin- the pretty fat chick before I lost over thirty pounds and the pretty thin chick after. This tickles me because people are so shallow. They think that what they see is all of me.

I have always had the highest esteem for myself and my journey. It is a part of the plan for my life. This evolution of my life is part of the vision I had years ago. My plan has always been to have my name in lights and this is only the beginning.

It's funny to me that when I walk in the door, people always ask, "How are you so confident that you are going to make it?" My answer is always the same, "Because I am a winner and winners never lose!" So, if I ever got 'no' as the answer, I always assumed it was not their final answer, or that they were not the right person to make the decision in reference to me. I would move on to find my 'yes.' Believing this way has never failed me. Your 'no' means nothing to me because it is in me to win.

There's a cost for everything, and I tend to pay more for the baggage that I'm already carrying. The issues, thoughts, and problems that I carry from my past don't travel with me free of charge. The fees of lost time and being frozen and being apprehensive because of things that I've experienced in life have been hefty loads to pay. That is why I decided to get rid of my baggage.

*Frequent and whole-hearted
laughter actually helps your
body to fight off harmful
diseases. By altering the levels
of cortisol in your body,
laughing lowers our levels of
stress and fights off things that
might be harmful to us.*

> **There's a luggage limit to every passenger on a flight. The same rules apply to your life. You must eliminate some baggage before.**

Rosalind Johnson

TWO

EXCESS BAGGAGE FEE

B efore I was a comedian, I worked at Taco Bell, Waffle House, Hardee's, and even Macy's as a teenager. I can happily say that those were the only fast-food and retail stores where I have worked. It was the worst, and neither the job nor the uniforms fit my vibrant personality, life plan, and style. I didn't like coming home smelling like chicken at all. I was tired of being tired and looking crazy. It was time for me to get my life together. No more minimum wage for this girl.

29

When I graduated from high school, I knew that I had to go to college to get to where I wanted to be. Besides, I was never given an option of not going to school, only the option of which school I would attend. I was committed to finding a better way of earning money while in school, so I soon found a job working in Corporate America as a software representative.

At seventeen years old, I made twenty dollars an hour as a product sales representative in retail stores, and it felt amazing. I literally talked people into buying what I was money," you do not know the entire story. Remember, comedians make a living telling half-truths. I wanted to know exactly how much they were getting paid, and I was determined to get it from the horse's mouth. I had come a long way since my sales representative position at age seventeen. Through the years, I climbed the corporate ladder and became a District Manager for Samsung Telecommunications which had the fourth-largest territory in the United States. I trained cell phone sales representatives for Verizon, AT&T, and T-Mobile. I was running things and worked hard to get every piece of each promotion, but I was not fulfilled.

Although that corporate check afforded my lifestyle, helped me buy my first home, and purchase a brand new six-series BMW, I began thinking more and more about my comedy ambitions. At this point, they were surpassing my corporate ambitions.

I started to hate my job, only loving my checks and the free stuff that came with being affiliated with the world-renowned Samsung brand. I remember doing a teleconference call in my gown with a blazer on top of it! I was so tired because I had been out all night. During the call, I received a private message from my co-worker saying, "Girl, we can see the ruffles from your gown! LOL!" Child, it had been one of those nights. I simply gathered myself together, closed my blazer, and continued to conduct business. Ruffles showing or not, I am a boss. So even with that mishap, I kept it moving. Business as usual.

Komedy Kocktails

I wrote my column until I worked up enough courage to perform on stage for the first time. It seemed like an undercover mission because I was hiding it from my day job and my co-workers. Even though I had big dreams and knew someday I would be a big star, I did not want them to fire me. Besides, I needed my job, and it was important to me to do and be at my best -- even while working for the man!

The day finally came in 2006. I took my dear friend Demetria's advice and tried my funny stories at an open mic. I was in Houston, Texas, at the Laugh Stop Comedy Club. I had no material or any idea where I would start, but I knew that I was something to see, and the people would love me! Well, at least that's what I kept telling myself. I got dressed, beat my face, jumped into Batman - yes, my BMW had a name - and drove to the club. I didn't know any of the night's performers, but they knew me because I had been around interviewing comedians. I signed my name on the list as "The Kiana Dancie" and when the guy asked why the

"The" I told him, "Because there's only one me!" He couldn't argue with my truth, so he said, "Oh, ok!"

When the host called my name, he said my name as I wrote it. "Coming to the stage, from Atlanta, Georgia, The Kiana Dancie!" I went on stage and talked about myself, and it was great! It was an amazing high. I was even asked to perform again, which meant that I was either good enough to command the stage or that I was at least funny enough to make people want to drink!

It was such a mind-blowing experience knowing I took a chance at stand-up comedy, and I was good at it. Now that I think about it, I have always been the person you would see on stage saying, "Kiana is hilarious, you never know what she's going to say next." Yes, I have to admit that that has always been me, and it was time to let that part of Kiana out for the world to see.

The decision to follow my heart could not have arrived at a better time. Pursuing comedy was a blessing because it allowed me to heal. I was carrying bags from my past relationships with Mr. 'No Go Pro' and Mr. 'I Can't Keep It In My Pants!'

I needed to do something different with my life; you know, shake things up. Comedy strengthened my confidence, giving me the motivation to keep pushing toward my goals, and it was working for me.

Ironically, my success as a comedian felt surreal but very natural. People actually liked my act, and it kept me in front of audiences, opening doors to bigger opportunities. A huge opportunity came in 2007 when I won a contest against a lot of veterans in the comedy community in Houston. This was a chance to open for actor and comedian Katt Williams. The prize was $1,000 for a ten-minute set. At the time, I didn't even have ten minutes' worth of material, but I was going to get that money!! I still can't believe that my first big show was to perform for an audience of seven thousand!! Not too many comics get that kind of exposure starting out. I knew I was on my way up.

I continued to push forward with my career, and in 2008 I was featured on 'Who's Got Jokes' with Bill Bellamy on the TV One network. I was also featured in a Cover Girl commercial, Queen on the Scene, with Queen Latifah and Eva the Diva. I went to L.A. for that opportunity and did my thing - making an impact in the comedy world.

To add fuel to the fire, my life was so crazy because I still had my corporate job. I thought my secret life on stage was safe until my boss called me and said, "Kiana, we saw you on TV." I can laugh about it today, but at the time, I knew my nice, cushy job was soon to be over. It was going to be a hard pill to swallow. So, reluctantly, I replied, "That wasn't me."

We both knew the truth, but I lied anyway. I was going to stick to my story. Then the unexpected happened. That boss of mine sent me a picture of myself on TV! I could not believe it. Here I am, busted by my boss, and all I could say was, "Well, I guess this is me! You got me!" LOL! Let's be honest. Towards the end of the role, I wasn't the best employee. I missed assignments and sometimes arrived late to meetings. It wasn't going well anyway. I'd been hearing that the team needed to be cut, and they would be letting people go. No one knew who would be a part of the cuts. Weeks later, on May 6th, 2009, my director called to tell me that they were cutting the team by fifteen percent, and I was a part of those cuts. I wasn't surprised, but my heart sank, danced, and even flipped. I couldn't tell if this was a blessing or a curse.

Although my director was very sad to let me go, he and I both knew I would be ok. To be honest, I probably would not have left on my own because I was holding on to that job for the coins. Honey, I was pushed out with my baggage on my back! They sent me packing with a nice severance package!

Some would say I took a leap of faith. I say it was a combination of being pushed and taking a jump at the same time. I was pushed because the job let me go. I'm educated and experienced, so I could have taken another job, but I didn't. I jumped right into my dreams! I always knew I was destined for greater, and I would have stayed at my job while trying to figure it out. I realized God had a different path for me to take and plan for my life.

My passion for doing comedy allowed me to heal from a bad breakup. God used the opportunity to speak to me and say, "Hey, it's now or never."

So, I declared, "I'm pretty, I'm funny, and I'm going to make it happen." I decided to move to Los Angeles, and yes, it was about to get real!

My motto became to hustle until you don't have to introduce yourself, and even then, somebody might not know you!

It Just Got Real

I remember sitting downstairs in the green room of the Houston Improv with a comedic genius that we all know. At the time, he wasn't talking to the press but sat down to talk with me. He explained why he walked away from his very successful show just as it was scheduled to air.

During production, he abruptly took a trip abroad, expressing his contempt for the entertainment industry's tone-deafness toward black entertainers and audiences. He continued to share his real feelings about the industry as we talked. The industry was asking him to do things that not only questioned his manhood but questioned him as a black man. I understood exactly what he was saying as this industry also questions me as a black woman. I've been on auditions where the will not to fail or allow anybody to tell me that I'm not good enough to succeed on my terms gave me a good reason to remove the bags from under my eyes.

In this competitive business, I needed to put my best face forward every time I went to work. I needed to make sure that I felt good about myself. Although no one has ever accused a stand-up comedian of being too pretty, the perception of Black female comics is that they can't be too attractive, or they won't be taken seriously. It's been said that Black women comedians should be fat, mammy-like characters. Well, that's too bad because I won't ever be that chick! When I walk on stage, the responses are always the same, "Wait, she's the comedian? Damn, she's pretty, and she's funny," as if that's impossible!

Looking back, I can definitely see the difference in me without the bags. I look like I've slept for weeks. I look younger. It's given me more confidence when auditioning, taking pictures, and even standing on stage looking pretty and acting funny.

From what I have been told and what I have seen so far, a girl needs to be extra secure while navigating this industry. It is rumored that the only way a female can get ahead in the comedy game is to screw her way to the top. I remember the first time I stepped foot in a Los Angeles comedy club, a comic told me, "Hey, you ain't gonna get nowhere by yourself. Let me help you. Come upstairs, 'cause all I need is fifteen minutes. I'll give you $1,500, and you can hit this fifteen-city tour with me."

I was blown away, but that would be the only thing that would get blown because that's an offer I did not take. If I were someone who was weak with no morals and did not have a strong family support system, I'm sure that I would have taken him up on that sorry-ass offer. Brand new in LA, not knowing anyone, or having a clear direction or clue of what to do next, I knew that I was not going to let this man tell me all he needed was fifteen minutes to get anything for me to be famous.

The sad part is that some girls fell for that. There are plenty of women in this industry who have screwed themselves just to get to the middle. Yes, I said the middle because they did not get to the top. The opportunities that came as a result of their shame were definitely not worth them giving up their sugar cookie. You must think about your self-worth. If I give myself away every time I get propositioned, then it's not so special. Second of all, I will eventually wear myself out. I have one vagina, and I need it for the rest of my life. I cannot let anybody run through me. If you devalue yourself, you are no good to yourself or anyone. I mean more to myself than that.

"We were filled with laughter, and we sang for joy. And the other nations said, 'What amazing things the Lord has done for them."

- Psalms 126:2

Laughter is its own universal language.

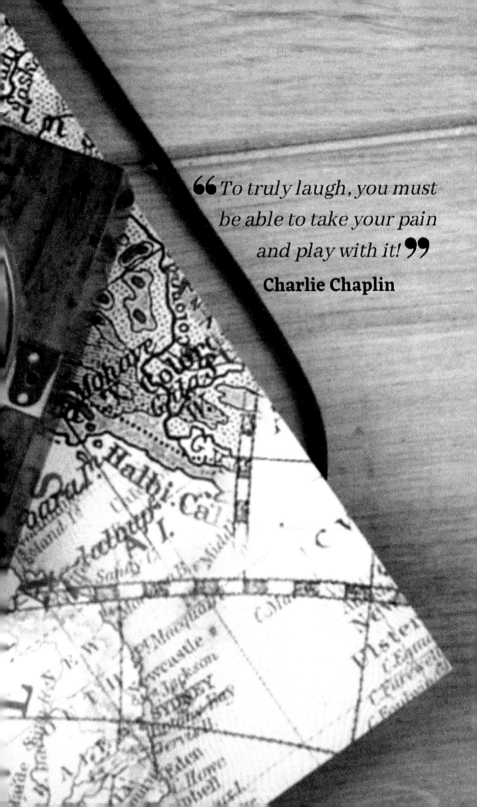

> **66** *To truly laugh, you must be able to take your pain and play with it!* **99**

Charlie Chaplin

Three

MOMMA DID NOTHING WRONG

A T six years old, I thought I was left with someone who cared for and regarded me in the highest way. I actually loved him, even though he took advantage of me and threatened my family.

He touched me. It was only once, but I knew it was wrong, and he threatened to harm my family if I told anyone. I didn't want anything to happen to me, my mother, or the rest of my family, so of course, I didn't utter a word. The fear I felt was not only real but, in my mind. It was larger than life because this actually happened in my own home. I was violated by a monster and not the kind that was under my bed or in my closet. It was a monster that my mama kissed when she left to go to work, a monster that sat down and ate dinner with us every day.

The monster lived in my home. A place I thought to be the safest place in the world for me where all things are good, and memories are warm and happy. Although it only happened once, it was still my reality. Oftentimes, people assume that the violator is someone unknown to them. However, this was not the case. It made me wonder how many times he thought about stealing my innocence before he actually had the opportunity to do it. I thank God I survived and had enough courage to say something.

Until recently, I have never spoken so candidly about my experience. I always felt it broke my mom's heart, but when I sat her down, she said, "Kiana, I want you to speak your truth! It hurts me more for you to have carried this as a part of your baggage. Share your experience. It may give others the courage to speak up. If you cut on the lights, you'll realize you're not the only one in the room."

I reminded her again, "Mama, you did nothing wrong. As a matter of fact, you did everything right. You left me in the care of someone you thought you could trust. You left me in the care of someone you had a relationship with. You left me in the care of someone who knew me, and who I knew."

She thought he loved us. So, the fact that he molested me was a great surprise and also a great disappointment. I am sure it never ran across her mind that he was even capable of this. The irony of the entire situation is that although she cared for him, she never once doubted me. Once I told her what happened, the next steps were immediate and intentional.

I remember it like it was yesterday. I usually have a foggy memory about a lot of things, but this one I remember. My mom kissed me goodbye and went to work. I laid down in her bed to feel more comfortable. My mother's room had a lot of windows, so it was very bright. Because I was so young, I could not stay home alone, so my mom told 'him' to stay with me. 'He' was her boyfriend of many years, but this was the first time my mom left me at home with him alone.

Then it happened. He touched me. When my mom returned home, I didn't want to tell her because of the threats he had made. I was young, impressionable, and yes, even terrified of what could have happened if I told. For weeks, I went back and forth on what to do. I went through every single detail of what happened that day trying to think of the best time to tell, but no time seemed right.

The perfect time came when there was an event at my school that addressed being touched inappropriately. That's when I told my teacher, Ms. Fadia, at Collinwood Daycare. I told her it happened to me. I wanted to be sure. I didn't miss one single detail that happened. Ms. Fadia was amazing! She was kind and fun. I trusted her and knew she would help me. I did not tell my mom at first because I was thinking about her safety. Thinking back, it was a very grown-up conversation that needed to happen.

After I explained what happened to me, Ms. Fadia called my mom. From there, my mom called the police, and they took Victor to jail. The end.

My mother was devastated, mainly because the molestation happened at the hands of a person she trusted. She thought Victor was trustworthy. He was around our family all the time, not someone we'd just met. My mom felt horrible as if she'd put me in harm's way because she didn't see that it was possible for Victor to hurt me. My mother started questioning her judgment, thinking she did something wrong. She needed reassurance that she did the best she could to protect me.

After Victor was arrested, he went to jail. I asked my mom how long Victor stayed in jail and she told me he didn't serve much time. That's the system we live in. We live in a system and society where people go to jail longer for selling weed than raping women, so I wasn't surprised when she told me about his punishment.

Miraculously, I have moved on and have healed from the situation. I thank my mother for her support. We have spent a lot of time crying, praying, and talking through what happened with a counselor. We loved each other through it, removing the shame from both of us. My mother let me know that it wasn't my fault and told me that she was sorry it happened. As much as my mother said we were blameless, I think she still carried a certain amount of guilt. She had done everything she could to protect me and give me an amazing life. She did her very best. For that, I am forever grateful.

Unpacking His Stuff

I do not remember if I ever had a moment where I felt dirty or wrong. I think I was scared and confused. I did not understand. I did not get it. I was a baby, a child, and Victor was a man, my mother's man, at that. My mom had been with him for years. It's nothing worse than being violated by someone you trust. We assume the people around us are there to protect us. Staying at home with Victor when I was sick with a fever, I assumed he was that person. Instead, he took advantage of his position and took away my innocence.

When I was molested, he took my naïveté from me without my permission. As a child, I did not know what sex was. I just thought I peed out of the thing. I knew boys kissed girls and maybe if she liked him, she kissed him back. Prior to Victor molesting me, I was a young, naive Catholic schoolgirl. I learned that life would be different. The comedian in me inappropriately laughs at the fact that I was molested at home versus at my Catholic school by the Priest! Maybe, I wasn't his type! Ok... I'll stop!

From that time forward, my family was very protective of me. They were very wary of who was around me and all the girls and boys in my family. My mother was very adamant about my healing process and how I would be as a young woman.

I release the bags I carry regarding my molestation every time I speak about it. It gives me a sense of relief because I understand that I'm not the only one. You know people that are dealing with this but they're not talking about it. People are afraid to tell their friends or family, thinking they will judge their actions or behavior, or place blame on them. Some people will think you actually did something wrong to warrant such advances.

In my case, I was six years old. I did nothing to make Victor molest me. For me, I couldn't think about what others thought. I have the strongest belief that we, as a people, have to stop worrying about what other people think. I think it's more important to share our stories. Oftentimes, when you share your fears, you learn that you aren't the only one who's afraid. My mom used to tell me all the time, "Never stop telling your truth."

Denying yourself the gift of healing will hinder your growth. I say, "Let go and let GOD!" And it feels good to let go of my bags. I didn't know the feeling of release would feel so good. When I look back, I say, "Wow, my life has been good, considering what I 've been through."

It would have been so much different had I not had the courage to open up and talk about what was going on with me! I'm so grateful!

To this day, I don't know where Victor is or what kind of life he lives. However, I do know he got out of jail. I often wonder if he learned his lesson. Has he touched another girl or boy? Has he committed any other crimes? Could he still be a molester? Did he escalate to a rapist? I hear that molesters often turn into rapists. I don't know, but

I'm so glad that being raped was not my truth. I've even wondered, does Victor even know who I am, because if he walked up on me, I wouldn't even know who he was.

Quite often, criminals don't believe they are wrong, and my assailant could still be bitter to this day. Victor could be mad about me putting him in jail. Will he run up on me one day? Those are real fears, but I've learned not to worry about that and just stay in prayer, remembering Isaiah 54:17, which says, 'No weapon formed against me shall prosper. And every tongue which rises against me in judgment, I shall condemn.' Although I curse sometimes, I still know my God and His Word. Please, don't get it twisted.

Despite my doubts, I can't and don't spend my days worrying about Victor because I serve a higher power, and I have plenty of things to do. I believe that God is always the one who takes care of me, including watching my back.

Some people dealing with molestation become bitter, questioning how God could let this happen to them. God doesn't necessarily let bad things happen. It's the way of the world. What happened to me was evil, but it didn't define me or stop me from believing in the greater good of life or God. It didn't define me that day, and it won't define me today or tomorrow.

I thought I was broken like my innocence had been stolen for good. I will forever be grateful to my mom for looking me in the face and telling me no one can take anything from me that I didn't give away. The only way Victor could have taken my innocence was if I allowed him to take it. Despite being scared and confused, the next day I woke up still a child. Despite my emotional scars and lack of understanding, I still wanted to play and do girly things. I still wanted to hang out with my friends and family and watch cartoons. So, regardless of what happened to me, nobody can take anything from me. That includes my innocence, spirit, and self-esteem.

I Still Believe in the Purity of People

When I wake up in the morning, I don't wake up and say, "Today I'm going to let somebody take my self-esteem," or "Today I'm going to let somebody take away how I see the world, positive or negative." I wake up with the assumption and the perception that life is going to be good, even to my detriment at times. I still believe in the purity of people. I still believe there are good-hearted people in this world. I believe that our differences make us amazing, that love heals all wounds, and that light will always shine!

It's a given that I'm going to have some sort of trust issues. I do have a very open heart, but also very protective about my space now. It's been said that I operate like I'm on an island alone and to that, I always reply, "Yes, that is true, and one day, I'll own one." The molestation did open my eyes to inappropriate behavior. When I see a man being too chummy-chummy or too friendly with children, it raises my radar. Although that innocence was lost, my heart is still pure when it comes to humankind.

If you or someone else you know is being threatened or harmed, please contact your local authorities, the National Sexual Assault Hotline at 1(800) 656-4673, or you may visit the

MeTooMVMT.org site for more information and resource to support yourself, a loved one or friend.

 For every fifteen minutes of solid full body laughing you do, you can burn up to 40 calories! Dieting? Get to laughing!

Little **Me** ...

"She is clothed with strength and dignity; she can laugh at the days to come."

- **Proverbs 31:25**

> **"** I've seen women who don't have great relationships with their dads, and it all comes down to this: You have to tell girls you love them every day. **"**

Chris Rock

Four

I GOT IT FROM MY DADDY

Before my father passed; we had a weird relationship. It was one of those situations where I questioned certain actions and never had the answers to make sense of things when you know something isn't quite right. My father and I would have crazy conversations, real grown conversations. I used to think to myself, "I'm a child, what are we talking about?"

He would say things like, "Baby don't sell yourself, but don't give yourself away either." I never knew what that meant, but as a teenager, those were the things we talked about. I guess in his own way, my father was sharing nuggets of wisdom, no matter how crazy it seemed. The things my father said to me when I was growing up make so much sense now that I am an adult.

My father never came to see me after my mom and I moved to Atlanta when I was nine. I wasn't just disappointed; I was actually very sad. My mom was from Cleveland and that's where she met and fell in love with my father. My mom gave birth and then it was over. She told me he never came to see me in the hospital. He never told her not to have me, but he wouldn't have received the father of the year award, either.

After my mom had me, my father and I were in and out of each other's lives. He was also in and out of jail. He would write letters or call me collect, and in some way, he was always around. I could remember that if I ever needed to speak to my father, I would have to call my paternal grandmother, or my Uncle Pie, his brother. They were literally the only people on Earth who knew where my father was on a consistent basis. It wasn't like I didn't have a relationship with my father because I did; it was simply strained.

In my opinion, he was irresponsible and simply inconsiderate. He was a very flamboyant, fashionable, well-spoken, and well-read man. He always had a new girlfriend or wife. I have never known him to have a job, but he stayed clean as a whistle!

I would go to Cleveland, Ohio, to spend summers with my father and I can count the number of times he was there with me at night. I spent most of my time with my mean aunt, Kathy, or my grandmother, which was a very interesting experience in itself. He would leave me with them versus spending time with me like he should have been.

When I turned thirteen, I told my dad, "This is the last time I'm spending the summer with you because I got things to do, and it's not to be locked up in the house with granny or your sister, Kathy! You ain't stuntin' me, and I ain't stuntin' you." Yes, in the south, "stuntin'" is a real word! In translation: I'm not studying you or paying you any attention. Plus,

I didn't like the way he lived, being here today or over there tomorrow!

My grandmother had roaches in her house, and that was enough for me. I decided I couldn't be there. They thought I was 'funny- acting' and they were right! I was choosy. I can't apologize for wanting to be in an environment where people can understand and cater to my standards. So, at thirteen, I decided I would spend my last summer in Cleveland because my dad lived below my standards, and I couldn't stay there anymore. That may have been harsh, but it wasn't like my dad was crushed about my decision anyway. If he was, he sure as hell didn't show it or tell me.

I packed my bags and went to my aunt's house and even that was an experience for me. My aunt had plenty of children, six to be exact, and I was an only child. It tickled me every time I went over there because the food they ate always came in black and white packages that I had never seen before. I used to call home telling my mom, "Ma, all of their food has blank names and comes in black and white packages. I don't know who makes this stuff!" She'd laugh so loud and say, "Girl, that's because it's generic!"

Honey, I was perplexed! My food had colors and names that I could read and recognize. My aunt and her children would clown me, calling me bougie because I didn't know about the off-brand food. My mom fixed that real quick, honey. She sent a box of food for me like I was away at college.

I like Heinz ketchup and French's mustard! I eat Jif peanut butter and Sargento cheese. I liked Frosted Flakes with the tiger and Kool-Aid, not Cool Drink! I don't know anything 'bout those other brands. Don't judge me! Ok, you can if you want, but I don't care! My aunt would tell me, "You'll eat all this fancy food, but when your food runs out, you can starve waiting on a box from your mama!" LOL!

The Dirty, Dirty

I am so glad that my mom decided to move south to Atlanta, Georgia. I believe that it was the most pivotal and the best decision she could have ever made. It's my opinion that the move allowed her to really open her heart and mind to the better things that life had to offer her. We wouldn't be who we are today had she not stepped out on faith! I asked her what made her move to Atlanta, and she said, "Well, your cousin Renee and I came down to Atlanta on vacation. In my mind, I already knew that I wanted to move."

Her confirmation came after reading an article in Ebony magazine about a very popular, successful news anchor named Monica Kaufman, whom I actually met in person. She was everything I thought she'd be - regal, pretty, and very warm. She was the "It Girl" in Atlanta. She had the trifecta going on - young, black, and respected! My mom was convinced that if this lady could do it, so could she! So, we moved to the land of milk and honey, where black folks ran the city.

My mother and I have lived in Atlanta, Georgia, for almost thirty years, and my father never stepped foot in Georgia on my behalf. He preferred to call and ask about my life rather than come to experience life with me. I had long gotten over what he wasn't going to do. I knew he was doing the best with what he was working with, which was very little.

I looked forward to having my father in my own space and fixing him a plate while we chatted about who knows what. But I never got the opportunity. I never had a chance to sit down with him to have a conversation in my own house. There were many things my father and I never got to do. Although my father wasn't involved in my life as much as I wanted, I can't deny the fact that he was in my life. I was told he suffered from alcoholism, although I never saw him drunk myself. I knew that he was fighting some type of demon; like many of us, he was in denial.

It's Just Different

I remember being one of the only cousins that traveled regularly. Every year we went on vacation multiple times, even traveling abroad. My mother would always say, "You'll be able to at least say, 'I've been to Niagara Falls.'" It was right there across the lake! Jesus!

Even shopping experiences were unique. My mother planned trips to go school shopping. Who does that? Traveling to New York, Los Angeles, or Pennsylvania, depending on her budget because Pennsylvania didn't charge taxes on clothing. It was always a treat. Even though I went to a private school, I would have all the cutest outfits because I had to be cute on the weekends. People would turn their noses up at places like New York. They'd say, "Oh, you went to New York to go shopping? Why? What's wrong with clothes in Cleveland." And later, I was asked the same about Atlanta. I had a very, very good childhood.

At an early age, I understood the type of environment I wanted to be in, and my father's standard of living was nothing I wanted to maintain as my normal. He seemed so unstable, bouncing from place to place. He appeared to be ok with it. As a small child, you don't notice the little details. You just accept the conditions and say this is family. But turning thirteen gave me the confidence to express what I didn't like, and I took advantage of the opportunity to do so.

As a child, I questioned my dad's actions, but I never felt like I could address them with him. I was either too young, or it would be disrespectful, so I kept my mouth shut. My mom made sure I always had the best of things and that I was loved and cared for. I believe all girls with absent fathers are, and I put those feelings away like many others. My father was a telephone dad. I wondered why he was so damn busy that he couldn't come to visit me, but, you know, it is what it is. At least I had some sort of a relationship with him and, more importantly, with my grandfather.

Daddy Issues?

You know, I don't know if I've ever really dealt with my father not being around consistently. I put those feelings away in my bag and kept living life, unaware of the real damage it could cause. I never had beef with my father. I knew he loved me but was only able to do so much. He gave when and what he could, although it was never enough. My mother made sure I felt loved, protected, and secure as much as possible, while my father played the "I'm here, but not here" role. Having my grandfather around allowed me to be raised by a loving man in my life.

I guess that was one of the hardest things I had to deal with in my life. I didn't even feel any pain when my father died. My father had a lot of women around him. I made up my mind that I was not going to spend time with him because he didn't have time to spend with me. To my knowledge, he was an alcoholic and forever in and out of prison. I was never given any true answers to why he went to jail, but I know it wasn't for the child support he never paid!

I vaguely remember him pulling a Mike Tyson move. Yes! He got into a fight with a man and bit off his ear! What an idiot! For some time, he would write to me with lots of promises that he would later break and later try to fix with gifts. It had gotten to the point where I didn't want to write to him. Like, why am I writing to you in jail? I'm not in jail. I was young and not interested in hearing his sob stories about his mistakes. My mom was a trooper; never once did she talk bad about him or his lifestyle.

I used to say to myself, "Why am I sitting down, spending time writing you letters because you got your silly self locked up?" And even to this day,

I don't date guys who have those kinds of issues. If you go to jail and we are together, then we broke up. I'm not that girl! I tell guys that I date, "If you're thinking I'm going to put some money on your books, or write you some letters, or kiss you in jail, nope, I'm not doing that." That has defined some of the things I will and won't accept. If you go to jail, you're on your own.

When I look back at our relationship, it wasn't all bad. However, it completely fell apart after my grandmother passed. When my grandmother was living, my relationship with my father was so much better. She was the glue that kept us as connected as we were.

Now, She's Dead

It seems so surreal that my grandmother is dead. For whatever reason, I always thought that she would be around. I remember it like it was yesterday. When my grandmother passed, I knew that keeping up with my father would be nearly impossible. I could always count on my little grandmother to know where her son was. The circumstances of my grandmother's passing are vague to me, but I do remember the day when I got the news that she was sick. I would call them at least every two weeks. 'Them," as in whoever answered the phone at my granny's house because they never called me. Sometimes, it would be my granny, my Aunt Kathy, Uncle Pie, or to my ultimate surprise, my father who answered the phone. I was told that she was sick and wouldn't be around much longer. I'll be honest, that's all I remember. I can't even remember if I went to the funeral. This is my truth, and yes, it hurts.

He's Dead, Too

My father dying also surprised me, but ironically enough, I didn't cry one tear. He was another one that I thought would be around forever. When my father passed on June 28, 2013, I did not go to the funeral. It was not that I did not want to go, but his evil sister did not let me know where and when he was being buried. I knew nothing, and I was not going to chase them to get it. If you do not want me to know where the man is being laid to rest, then so be it. I find that family can be so petty. I spoke to his wife for hours, and she made it clear to me that they, his sisters, were making it impossible to plan for his funeral.

I was on the way to Cleveland to attend his funeral, but something in me said, don't go if you're at peace with not going. So, I didn't go. I talked it over with my mom's side of the family and Jesus and kept it moving! I can't make people do right, so why try? My mom and I got together and laughed at some of the good times we remembered about my father. We then visited our family and celebrated his life.

"Blessed are you who weep now, for you shall laugh!"
- Luke 6:21

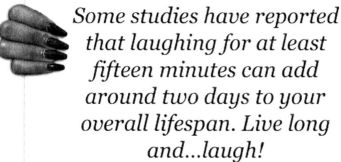

Some studies have reported that laughing for at least fifteen minutes can add around two days to your overall lifespan. Live long and...laugh!

The Kiana Dancie

Baby Me ...

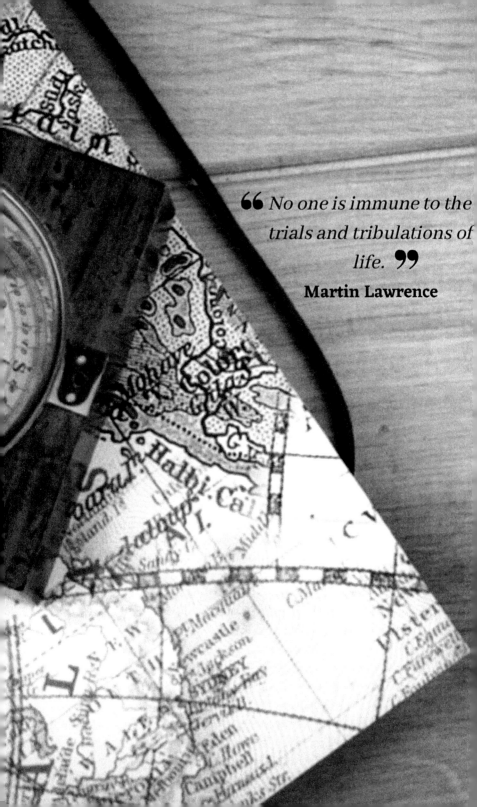

❝ *No one is immune to the trials and tribulations of life.* **❞**

Martin Lawrence

Five

THE NIGHTMARE NO-ONE SAW COMING

In my junior year of high school, I needed to play catch up or I would not graduate on time. To catch up, I attended Open Campus High School in Dekalb County which was created for students who had situations like mine. I had to take Spanish 1 and Spanish 2 that school year, so I could graduate with my class of '96. It was a Spanish overload, but I was determined. I thought it was so crazy that my Spanish teacher was a Black lady, but she was really cool, and she knew her stuff! She had traveled the world as a Spanish teacher and had all the stories and experiences that really intrigued me.

So, here I am in Spanish class, talking to one of my classmates about my upcoming prom, discussing the details - my dress, where I wanted to eat, and most importantly how we were going to get there, as there was a group of us going together. Then this guy named Charles, whose name has been changed for the sake of this story starts talking about how he missed his prom.

He asked, "When is your prom?"

Not thinking anything about it, I replied, "My prom is coming up in a week."

He looked at me and my girl and said, "I'll take you; I got my license and a car." DING! DING! DING! That was the correct way to butt into a conversation!

As he was talking about taking us to prom, my girl and I were trying to figure out how we would tell my boyfriend that this random dude from Spanish class was taking us to prom. At the time, my boyfriend could not get off from work no matter how hard he tried. He was older than me and had a real job as a manager at a local U-Haul store. Since he was a manager, no one wanted to cover his shift, and that meant no prom date for me.

After considering his offer and the benefits of him taking us to the prom, I made sure I told him, "Well, you know I have a boyfriend, but my boyfriend won't trip if you want to go."

Again, not thinking anything was funny about his offer, we decided that day in class that he would be our escort and he would drive US to the prom! We were excited and going as a group was perfect! We could have fun being young and free, living out the remaining days of our junior year without the pressure of 'prom night.' It was strictly platonic. We did not even coordinate our colors. My dress was purple. My friend's dress was green. He wore black so providing a corsage was unnecessary. The entire night we operated as friends. I paid for my dinner and my friend paid for hers. We did not dance or hold hands. That was not an option. Not one time did he act like he was our 'date' for the evening. In fact, I don't even know if people knew he drove us to prom or was a part of our group.

Despite the circumstances, we had a great time. It was a night to remember. I wish I could have held onto that memory instead of the nightmare that was to come.

We stayed until the prom was over and then headed back home after eating breakfast. Of course, no night of partying in Atlanta is official if it doesn't end at Waffle House! We dropped my homegirl off first, right before curfew and since my house was the furthest, I was the last to be dropped off. He seemed cool and respectful. He didn't try any funny business with me or my friend. The one thing that I noticed was that he stopped a few times at the gas station and bought a little bottle of something that I had never seen before. It had a scorpion or a worm in the bottle. It was weird, and I assumed it was an energy drink because he didn't reek of alcohol or act differently. So, I didn't make a big deal out of it.

Even though I enjoyed myself, I was excited about seeing my boyfriend the next day! I was so excited to tell him all the details and even show him the pictures when I finally got them. The ride home was basically silent, although we did make some small talk. But for the most part, it was crickets, and I was okay with that. We did not talk much in Spanish class either, so I was not expecting a lengthy conversation on the way home.

When we arrived at my house Charles said he was tired. I could imagine he was tired from driving all over metro Atlanta. Besides, I lived in Chamblee, Georgia, at the time and he lived deep on the other side of town in Decatur, Georgia, which was at least a thirty-five-minute drive away.

He was like, "Man, I don't think I can drive home. Can I lay down for a second?" It was three o'clock in the morning, so I understood how tired he must have been. I empathized with him. He wanted to take a short nap and get up in about an hour to drive home to Decatur. It seemed harmless at the time. I mean, after all, he did take my friend and me to the prom. Although I knew it wasn't the right thing to do, all I could think of was him running off the road due to falling asleep. So, I let him lay down.

Honestly, I felt safe enough to oblige, even though it was the first time my mother ever left me at home alone. Why she did on this night, I do not know. She and my brother went over to my stepfather's house on the other side of town. It was very, very weird, and highly unusual that she was not home, ESPECIALLY ON PROM NIGHT!

I agreed to let him come inside and lay on the sofa. Being tired myself, I walked to my bedroom to rest on the bed. I knew that I couldn't go to sleep too hard, or it would be trouble in the morning. My bedroom window didn't lock and the only two people in the world that knew that were my beloved boyfriend, Eric Lovejoy, and myself. It seemed like I had only been lying down for five minutes before I heard tapping on my bedroom window.

I already knew it was Eric wanting to climb through the window as he had done on several occasions. My mother would kill me if she knew how often this happened. Since the window did not lock, it was easy for Eric to sneak in whenever we wanted. But tonight, was different. Charles was still on the sofa in the living room. I had expected him to be halfway near Decatur by now, but instead, he was snoring on my couch. I could not let Eric be surprised by seeing him lying there in my living room, so I went to the window and said, "Hey come to the door and I'll let you in."

Eric must have wondered why I wanted him to go to the door instead. I am sure he saw the dude's car parked outside the house and made a whole lot of assumptions. I know he was confused about whom the car belonged to, so I just opened the door. I often wish that I had never opened the door and had figured out a way to lock the window and let him either try to open the window or knock on the door. Man, I wish...

I did not want Eric to be upset that this dude was still at my house. He was fully aware of him taking me and my girl to the prom, and he expected him to be gone. I had to let my boyfriend know that Charles was there before he came inside the house.

Staring directly at Eric, he said one sentence, "You gonna disrespect me and you couldn't even take your bitch to the prom?!"

And in that instant, he raised his arm and pulled the trigger of the 22-caliber gun that he was apparently carrying with him all night! I was in shock. I HAD NO IDEA!

Before I could process what was happening, shots were fired – BOOM, BOOM, BOOM! "What just happened?" I thought. Once I opened my eyes, I saw Eric laying on the floor.

He shot my boyfriend! "OH, MY GOD! HE SHOT ERIC!" I screamed.

Charles began walking around in a circle. I assume he was trying to figure out what he was going to do now, and what he was going to do with me. I knew it was only me and Jesus Christ that could save me, so, I started talking.

The other thing my father gave me was a mouthpiece. I was known for being quick-witted and had a way of getting whatever I wanted out of the deal. He always told me, "You could talk your way out of any situation." And it was true because I had seen and heard him do it on several occasions.

My father was one of the smoothest, most charismatic men I have ever met in my life. He always had a way with words, and it seemed like I picked up on his gift instantly. His best advice:

"Sometimes you have to talk it out, so you can change the temperature of the situation."

As a comedian, I practice that advice when I come up with new material, sometimes on stage, with a rowdy crowd staring at me, I have to always be ready. The audience would be ready to throw tomatoes at me at any sign of unfunniness! It was no wonder I perfected the gift of gab I inherited from my dad.

Very calmly and suggestively, with a very specific goal of saving my life, I began telling him that the neighbors probably heard the gunshots, and he should leave before they called the police. It would be one of the most important conversations of my life, one that could determine if my mom and little brother would come home to two dead bodies lying in the living room. I had to use this mouth to talk him off of the ledge, and yes, prevent him from shooting me.

As I was talking to Charles, he continued to walk around in circles, waving his gun in the air, talking to himself, looking, and sounding crazy, all at the same time. Eventually, he walked out of the door, still talking crazy to himself. Scared and confused, I ran to the door and locked it. I called 911, as well as my mother, and told them what happened. It was still so unbelievable to me. I just couldn't believe what just happened. My mouth just saved my life.

I don't like the word trauma, but it's the only word to describe the nightmare of watching my boyfriend lie on the living room floor that night, suffering from a gunshot wound to the stomach. It was a traumatic situation, and at that moment, I realized how precious life was. Not that I didn't know it already, but holding my boyfriend on the floor, waiting for the ambulance, has a way of putting things in great perspective. I held him, not knowing if I would be lying there next to him at any moment. The man that shot my man had left the house in a frenzy, and yes, I was terrified! Maybe he'll come back! Maybe he'd burn the house down! I was petrified! As Eric lay on the floor in my arms, I whispered in his ear that I was sorry, that I loved him, and that the ambulance was on the way.

It seemed like the paramedics and police arrived at the same time. Eric was still moaning and groaning on the floor when they loaded him on the stretcher. He was still alive, but they would not allow me to go to the hospital with him. The police had a million questions for me.

I was told later that my baby Eric died on the way to the hospital. Damn, Eric! DAMN! I was supposed to be Mrs. Lovejoy! Damn!

The What If's

I often wonder if I missed something. Were there signs that I or my friends missed throughout the night? Clearly, Charles was upset after Eric told him he had to leave, but I did not think he was that pissed off. Prom night was all about having fun as friends. I did not make Charles think that we had something going on. I did not give him the impression that there was a possibility that he and I could get together. The more I look back on it, this was clearly a typical 'who had the biggest ego in the room' thing. This was some 'man versus man' stuff that I could not and would never understand.

One thing I learned from that situation - bruised pride is a mutha!

The struggles I went through yesterday made me who I am today.

I watched my boyfriend get shot in my house, and I held him in my arms while he was dying. That showed me that you could literally be here today and gone tomorrow in a split second. There was not even that much blood. I honestly thought we were going to the hospital where my boyfriend would pull through, and we would talk about it the next day. But that did not happen. In one night, I lost the love of my life.

That event changed me forever. I do not recall if I went back to school the next day, but I do remember not wanting to sit in the house. I needed to get out. Idle time played tricks on my mind. Even though I knew there was nothing I intentionally did to make Charles act that way, thoughts began to fill my head that made me believe that maybe I sent some kind of wrong signal.

I asked my friends if Charles was flirting with me and if maybe I was too friendly. Was it because we didn't dance together? All of us danced in a group, so there was no one-on-one dancing. I was his homegirl, we were all just cool. At least, that's what I thought! A fun night turned into a nightmare nobody saw coming.

Charles was arrested and sent to jail. In fact, he is still in jail to this day. I think a few years ago, he came up for parole and of course, my family contested so he is still locked up. The crazy thing is that I did not even know the man had a gun. I did not know people who walked around with guns, especially at seventeen years old. I guess I did; I just was not aware.

I do not know why he had a gun in the first place or why he felt the need to use it that night. Maybe he thought that he was protecting me. I know he did not like the way Eric was talking to him. All I know is there was a room with two alpha males and apparently Charles felt disrespected when Eric woke him up and asked him to leave.

Here, you have a dude standing in my boyfriend's face teasing him saying, "You couldn't take your girl to the prom and now you talking junk to me telling me to get the hell out of here?"

Then, you have Eric meeting the man that took his girlfriend to her prom. He's tired after working all day. He's wondering why this man is asleep on his lady's couch, and now he just wants him to get out. The first-time dude walked out, he should have just stayed out there, but he could not, because he felt like his manhood was bruised and that Eric punked him. I will always remember that people take being disrespected seriously.

"I will turn their mourning into joy, I will comfort them and give them gladness for sorrow." —
Jeremiah 31:13

Bulging Baggage

It was a lot going on that night. The hardest thing for me was calling our mothers to tell them what happened, especially since it was my first time being home alone. I did not want my mother to question or judge herself. I am thankful my mother did not come home to find two dead bodies on her living room floor.

Explaining what happened to Eric's mama was even harder. Calling a mother in the wee hours of the night to tell her that her baby was shot and killed was one of the hardest things I ever had to do. Although I did not pull the trigger, it felt like I did. The last thing I wanted was for Eric's family to be mad at me or blame me, which I know they did and still do. They were not there so they do not know exactly what happened. Honestly, they did not even care about what happened; all they knew was that Eric was gone and I was one of the last people to see him.

I talked to Eric's sister a few years ago and she was still grieving, understandably. I felt she was still angry with me and I know she was still hurting. I guess she felt like she lost a big brother, whereas I only lost a boyfriend. My loss doesn't compare to hers. The truth is she did lose a big brother and there is nothing I can do to make that feeling go away.

I carried the baggage of thinking it was my fault for a long time. Through counseling, a lot of prayers, and God carrying me through, giving me the strength to forgive, I pushed forward. I was able to forgive dude. I had to forgive him to heal. It was not easy. I forgave him, but I never forgave myself. The thing about forgiveness is that it is hard to do no matter how much you pray about it. I had to ask God to give me the strength to endure it, and it was done.

When you decide to push through all the drama and hardest obstacles of your life, all the elements in the universe speak to that energy. God will hear you. He will know the bags you carry and give you the courage and strength to let them go and move forward.

This tragedy made me become a more transparent person. I don't want to be played with or misled, so I'm definitely not going to play with you. It altered the way I interact with people and changed my approach to relationships. I made sure that everybody knew what the deal was with me. I became very open about my feelings when it came to dating.

Before Eric was murdered, he wanted me to go to college and get a good education. He had all these plans for us, and I believe they would have happened if he were still alive. We probably would have gotten married.

He sat down with my mom and said, "I know I'm twenty and Kiana is seventeen, but I want her to go to school." I loved and cared for him so much, and I still do. I knew we would have a happy life together after I finished school. After he was killed, I didn't want to go away to school, but my mother was not playing with me.

She told me, "I'll buy you a car if you go away to school." That was motivation enough to keep me moving forward in life and to continue to heal. So, honey, I enrolled in Georgia Southern University, and I was off to school in the Fall of 1996.

Believe it or not, there really is a science to laughing. In fact, the science of laughing and its effects on the body is referred to as Gelotology.

> **"** *I DON'T have EX's! I have Y's. Like 'Y the hell did I date you?!* **"**
>
> **Kevin Hart**

Six

I THOUGHT HE WAS GOING PRO

When it comes to relationships, I believe that time is short, so you have to get your life together and be honest about your feelings and expectations. I'm not going to just hang around here if you can't provide what I need as a man. I'm not going to waste time with you because each day I have less to give away and I never know if today is my last. I'm not rude, but I do let people know what I need so we are all on the same page.

I learned that lesson from having a long-term relationship with a guy I met in college who I thought was headed to the NFL. I invested in him, wanted the best for him, and thought we would get married, but it was not so. For as long as I can remember, I've always been crazy in love with boys. I have always had a boyfriend and I have always been a one-man-at-a-time type of lady. I was always in a long-term relationship, a serial monogamist. But that is not always a good thing, especially when you feel the time spent with that special someone is a big waste.

At nineteen, I met a young man named Joseph. It was the typical love story - we met in college, fell in love, and I ended up being with him for ten long years! Yes, I said TEN long years! What do you know about that decade love? LOL! The love story had a few wrinkles though. I should have seen the signs of a bad relationship in the making. I knew he wasn't ready when I met him. He was gorgeous and athletic. All the girls wanted him. That was part of the problem - too many girls chasing after my boyfriend.

I remember the first time Joseph came over to my house. One of his girls followed him and knocked on my door. She had the nerve to tell me he was her boyfriend. I politely replied, "Well, he may be your boyfriend, but he's at my house now. So, you have to wait 'til he leaves!" This is how it was all the time. I slammed the door in the girl's face and turned to him for an explanation for the interruption. While I prepared to play the tiniest violin in the world, he told me he had dated her in the sixth grade and that they had a long-term puppy-love relationship. Here we are in our third year of college and this dude was talking about sixth-grade relationships. I knew then what it was all about, and I should have walked away, but I didn't. He was a player, but honey, players get played. So, I tiptoed around that game carefully! Well, at least I tried.

Joseph was a great football player and all the signs pointed to him going into the NFL. Muscular and charming, he was one of Georgia Southern's finest! I liked him a lot, but unfortunately, I wasn't the only one who liked his big ass! We came from very different backgrounds so I thought I could influence him to be a better person. I came from a good family, with a strong mother and an amazing foundation. I always had money in my pocket and had always known the better things in life. He also came from good people and had amazing people supporting him, but it was different. VERY Different.

Knowing this, I wanted to share my experiences with him. I was happy to share my gifts, talents, and other things I knew to help make him a better person. Joseph was working in the cafeteria on campus, and I told him, "That's not any money; you work too hard for your coins." I knew how to make money and I showed him how to do the same. Although he was smart and a great athlete, he only had one plan, to make it to the pros. He had the raw goods, but he didn't know how to utilize them to execute a plan.

When I met him, he had a baby on the way. Lord, had I had any sense, I would have RUN AWAY! I don't care if you're a student. I don't care if you get food out of the cafeteria or wherever it comes from, you now have to get it together to take care of a whole baby! When I learned that he had someone else depending on him, I did not understand why he lacked the hustle that I knew he needed to possess to take care of his responsibilities.

He was content with being the athlete known as 'Big Joe.' I didn't think he should keep showing up empty-handed. I showed him how to make money and got him together quickly. At least, I thought I did.

I introduced him to several ways to make money while in school, but I soon realized no matter how much I wanted it for him, I could not make him want it for himself. He was a true athlete with not only hopes but the skills to really play professionally. After blowing out his knee playing basketball with his boys, he was devastated, and I was, too. I had invested a lot into this man and now the dream has shifted.

Ok, I can adjust, and I was determined to stand by him to help him deal with the feelings of failure and his dreams of being a professional athlete being destroyed. He had to be willing to hustle, and he did not have it in him.

I Gave Him Ten Good Ones

I never thought I would fall in love again after Eric. But then, I met Joseph and I liked our love story. I truly thought we could have a good life together.

I was with that man for ten years, constantly helping him find a job, begging him to be faithful, and fighting with his baby mamas. Yes, I said mamas. That was getting old. I thought the dude would get it together, but it was the same old news. I won't lie. We broke up literally every week, and even stayed broken up for as long as a year, but we always managed to get back together.

I never understood what our attraction was, but it was crazy how we couldn't stay apart. Joseph had his own baggage, too. We often say that women are broken, but there are many broken men out there, too. He was adopted by his grandparents because his mother was in no condition to raise him or his brother, and his father was incarcerated. We shared similar stories about our fathers with each other. It meant a lot to both of us, and we definitely had a bond. We relied on each other for support, although my father had been out of jail for a long time. I could not deny our connection at that moment.

Even though Joseph cheated on me, I could relate to his feelings about his father. I loved him and although neither one of us was perfect, we tried to make it work. There eventually became a time when I could not take it anymore. The negatives outweighed the positives, and he was not trying to change for me. I know y'all are wondering, 'Does he need to change for me, or for himself?' Well, the answer is for ME if I'm going to be in his life. Hence the reason why I walked away.

I did everything I could to help him become a better person, not only for himself but also for me. Child, I cooked, shopped, prayed for and over him, I nursed him, I stripped for him, I was his cheerleader, his trainer, his counselor, his trainer, his assistant, his housekeeper, his child support attorney, I paid all our bills – you name it, I did it! However, there was a limit. I will always love myself more than any man walking. After ten years, I realized he was not going to get his life together and I decided I was not going to play games. It was time to move on. Years of trying to help him get established failed because he just could not keep a job. Blowing out his knee was traumatic for him, and I honestly believe he was depressed. His dream of playing professional sports was over and he did not have a Plan B, unlike me. Even Walmart sold Plan B's – I know, I've bought a few!

He did not know what he was going to do, so I made sure I did everything I could to help him find work that would allow him to take care of us in the future. I was very supportive because I believed he had it in him, a mistake many women probably make that becomes baggage. I even supported him in wanting to play semi-professional football.

The last straw was when I helped him get a job making $15,000 a month -- non-taxed -- and he lost it! I never got a clear answer on how he lost that good job, but all I did know was that I was DONE! How do you lose that kind of job? All you have to do is show up. He was the boss, and he was getting paid. One thing that I've learned is you can't make a man work, no matter what. If he doesn't want it, he won't do it!

I understood his original plan did not work, but you have to always be open to exploring other options. When I was helping him find work, I found myself thinking, 'Well you're not going to play in the league, but you can still make a substantial amount of money.' Fifteen thousand a month for a young man with two kids and a girlfriend clearly could have been a great setup for the future. When he screwed that up, all I could do was walk away.

After getting laid off from Samsung, I packed my bags and moved to L.A. to pursue my dreams of becoming a comedian. I needed that time to heal. That was my final breakup with him. We had broken up a million times before, but this time, I was done.

I Gave Away My Twenties

I struggled with the fact that I stayed with my ex for ten years. I think this was mainly due to the fact that I gave 1000% of myself, but he didn't do the same. I had to sit down and re-evaluate my life. I was able to really put things in perspective. From that day forward, I stopped looking backward at the time I spent and started looking forward at the time I would have wasted if I had not walked away. My future looked bright, and it was up to me to drop that 'I gave away my 20's' baggage!

Now that I am older, I am fully aware of my ability to control my future and even influence my relationships. I am coming to the part of my life where I want to have kids, but not without a husband. I have NO desire to be a single mother. I am not judging, but baby, I don't want it to be that way. I know that life happens, and there are some things you can't control. I feel that I am worthy of a husband, the picket fence with the house in the cul-de-sac, some babies, and yes, even a few dogs.

It's crazy that I have begun thinking that I may have overlooked a great guy that wanted to pursue me because I was so focused on other things and other people such as the ten-year guy. Smh! I guess that is the quandary of any relationship, and the risk we take when we make an emotional and physical investment in anyone. There's always a chance your investment will not pay a return, which usually feels like you are losing.

Lately, when I'm looking at social media, a lot of guys that I have dated are getting or already married. It's hilarious to me, LOL! I like to say that I was the prepping camp for them. I am a strong believer that when a man is ready to find his wife, he finds his wife. Maybe I have met my husband, but he was not ready. He may have met his wife and I was not ready. Who knows? I don't have a crystal ball to see the future or the past. All I can say is that my husband is being prepared for me and he'll find me soon enough. I also believe that if I have met my husband and it was meant for us to be together, then he will come back to get me. That's something I have to accept.

A lot of my girlfriends are now going through life changes like getting married and having babies. I laugh because I don't even have a boyfriend. I will admit that I am way too picky and haven't made any real attempt to have a man. The guys that are pursuing me haven't sped up that attempt at all. They aren't that serious and to be honest, I believe they are intimidated by me.

I cannot help but wonder if my attention was in another direction and if these men felt that. Maybe others thought I was not serious, and I was not ready for real love or vice versa. I might have run a couple of good guys off. Knowing me, I probably did. Maybe they weren't good for me. I don't know. At this point, I'm not tripping on any of it.

There was a time when I was in my feelings about dating and breaking up with Joseph. I was with him for so long, and I was always thinking, who spends ten years of their life with a man who was not going to marry them? Clearly, I thought he was going to. In fact, he asked me to marry him multiple times. Basically, he was only grasping at straws. He knew that I was ready to leave him. He was right to feel it coming. When I finally packed my bags, I was good gone! I could have been doing so much more with my time but guess what? I wasn't.

Through that process, I learned that once I gave myself the opportunity to really think about what happened during our relationship, I became a much stronger woman. I also became such a better person because I knew what I should have known years ago. I now knew the BS that I am not going to take from anybody -- no matter who they were -- who your daddy is, who your mama is, or whom you have around you.

If I'm in your life, I'm the queen, and you will treat mc as such. I hear ladies say they do not do this and do not accept that from a man, but you do not know what you will and will not accept until you are in a situation where you have to decide. Now that I have unpacked that bag, I know what I know! A man must approach me the right way. Plain and simple. Old school, traditional approaches. If that's not you, get out my DM!

I gave my twenties away. My thirties were for a good time, and my forties, well, let's just say I'm not wasting any time. Before we go any further, let me clarify what I mean when I say my forties are not to be played with. At this moment in my life, I know exactly what I want. I'm not wasting time with anyone. We can go out to dinner, but there has to be a very specific goal because I'm not just dating; I can feed myself the finest meals! If you want a friend with benefits, I'm not her! Keep it moving! I'm a big girl now, and I'm not here for the games.

In my twenties, I did not know any better. I had YPD! I suffered from the Young, Pretty, and Dumb syndrome! Now, don't get me wrong, I've always been this girl, the forward, assertive, progressive, and driven person. Sometimes, I found myself wanting to not rock the boat. Now, I have NO cares to give!

When I met my ex at nineteen, I was already focused on my goals, and still mourning my last boyfriend's murder. My actions were very specific and calculated. I crack up all the time after thinking about how long I made him chase me. When we met, I said to him, "You'll never have me!" and walked away! Well, he clearly made me eat those words! Once he and I started dating, I had all intentions of making that relationship work, and I did everything within MY power to do so. In my opinion, that was to the detriment of my better judgment.

Even though I wanted my relationship to work, I told him and myself often, "I love me more than you, and I'll leave you in a blink of an eye!" I talked big stuff, and it literally took 1,000 breakups to reach the ultimate, "I'm done!" I learned that I'm ok being single.

I heard a sermon once and the pastor said, "Don't settle for breasts and britches," meaning do not have a woman or a man around only to say you have a man or a woman in your life. This is especially true if that person is not going to do right by you. That was my life with Joseph. I settled for arm candy, and he was so sweet he gave me cavities. He was not doing right by me. My friends called him, 'Mr. Can't Get Right!' We would all say the same thing, "He's fine, but he can't do right!!"

He was sweet as pie, and he gave me everything he had. He loved the very ground I stood on, but not enough to be faithful. I was a good woman to Joseph, and he will tell you that to this day. In fact, he called me not too long ago saying, "You don't want to get back with me, do you?" The words jumped out of my mouth before I could process what he was asking, "Boy, bye, and now go sit in the corner!"

Most importantly, I knew that although I was carrying some baggage from that relationship when I walked away, I am not my baggage. Once I acknowledged my bags, I dropped, unpacked, and yes, even burned them to allow myself to heal! I won't carry one more bag based on that failed relationship. I gave 1000% of myself and that was all I could do.

No More Looking Back

As women, we have to stop looking backward. A lot of women stay in bad situations because they do not want to be single, and they feel like they have invested too much time. This may be true a lot of the time. Emotions may have been invested, but, at the end of the day, if he's still not loving you, and I mean loving you and regarding you, not just making love to you, you might as well leave.

What are you staying there for? That's the question you must ask yourself. I had to ask myself that same question and it was difficult to answer. Because of my experience, I now have the wisdom of being in the game versus sitting on the bench.

I have earned the right to share with someone and say, "Hey, let me tell you what you need to do." If they are willing to listen, then I proceed to explain what I've been through. Straight to the point, I tell them, "You need to recognize that as baggage and let it go."

I let them know that I have been there and done that! I have the refrigerator magnet to prove it! I am speaking from experience rather than from what someone told me! Now every situation is different, but I try to always share my highs and lows so people can relate and know that they are not going through it alone!

I have met so many young ladies in relationships that are not going anywhere. But because she's in love or he's attractive and painting her a nice picture of the future, using the finest paint brushes and most expensive paints on borrowed canvas, she fails to see the truth.

It is a picture filled with promises while she is steadily packing her bags. Not bags that she can leave with, but bags that will hold her down! Filling them up with all his shortcomings, neglect, cheating scandals, lack of ambition, unfulfilled promises, and baby mama drama. She is oblivious to the weight of the drama-filled items she's packing for the journey that may not appear until six or seven years down the road when she is looking crazy, and the baggage begins to explode.

Some of the bags she's carrying may not explode; they may stretch to maximum capacity making them harder, but not impossible, to carry. Or literally, her bags are on the verge of bursting wide open! Usually, this happens at the most horrible time, with the wrong person. Now she is carrying her bags into every relationship in her life. She's a mess at home, hard to work with and clearly, if she's in a relationship, she gives her man hell because she is not happy and unwilling to address the real issues!

The guy has not asked to marry the girl. He continues to make false promises, and basically wastes her time, knowing that he has no intention of doing right by her. But she is so in love she can't see it. If she does, she's ignoring it. She may have even had his child, but he has not made her his woman.

He has not put her in front of his friends, family, and God. He has not said, "This is the one." I've seen it over and over again. I tell women all the time, if you see this situation, don't waste any time! Pull your sister-friend aside and tell her, "Uh-huh, girl, he gotta go!"

If a man really wants to be with you and marry you, it does not take him that long. What is he doing? It doesn't take that damn long to know if you have found a good woman, or if she isn't the one, then you should leave her alone. Don't be surprised if that sister-friend starts rolling her eyes and neck and telling you off, but you did right by her, even when her man couldn't and wouldn't.

I know a lady who is fifty years old, has been living with her man for years, and she still has not met his mother! He has had every opportunity to take her home to his mama's house, and my friend's defense is, "Well you know, we were supposed to go last year, but the storm hit, and this time he had something to do, so I didn't go." There is always an excuse, but she continues to justify this by saying, "I talk to her on the phone." My response is, "That is fine, but she still doesn't know you."

At the end of the day, he is not trying to bring you around his mother. He is not trying to let you know her because he's not that into you. If a man is really serious about you and is trying to marry you, he will bring you around his friends and family, especially his mamma.

Looking back at my own situation only makes me wonder what was wrong with my ex. I had met every single person in his life and still, to this day, I have a relationship with his grandparents. But like I said, he loved me, but didn't know how to do right!

The signs were there, but I chose to ignore them. I was a full participant in the BS. I say all the time that I enabled him. Remember, a week after I met him, his 'girlfriend' at the time, whom he'd been with since the sixth grade, was knocking on my door. It takes two to play the game. I'm not saying I wasn't without fault, but I did everything I could to do right by him. Despite everything, I allowed myself to stay in the situation believing that I could fix it, or he would eventually fix it himself. I did not know which one, but it was one of them.

I have learned that I cannot make anyone be with me if they do not want to be with me. I have learned that you cannot fix people; they have to want to change. I have learned that no matter how good you are to a person if they do not want you at that time, they are going to go looking for what they want, while you wait for something that is probably never going to happen.

Staying in my relationship with Joseph for so long was a lesson learned. I kept taking him back thinking he was going to change. I carried that bag of 'I hope my man changes into the right man' around with me for a long time. I am now more intentional about what I put in my bag. I see it all coming before I even pick it up. I do all I can to avoid it. I walk around it. I kick it away. I jump over it, but I won't pick it up.

Every now and again, however, I will say, "I didn't see that coming." Sometimes, you don't. Sometimes you're not able to see it. Honey, listen, he can smell good, have an amazing body with all his teeth, and appear to be the answer to all your dreams! He can speak well and do everything to get you while looking all nice and shiny, but still be a bum. Now, I pay extra close attention to more than how he looks. I look at how he walks, how he dresses, how he carries himself, and how he interacts with me and other people. I listen to every word that comes out of his mouth. People show you who they are every time, but we get distracted by other things, so we miss or ignore them. I won't ever get caught slipping again, I promise.

Once I determine if I want to be bothered with him, it's on. I know for a fact that my discernment will always tell me if he will waste my time. If he's really serious and ready to 'crown me' as his one and only queen, then he becomes my one and only king.

"A time to cry and a time to laugh"

- Ecclesiastes 3:4

Just as children laugh more than adults, surveys have shown that women tend to laugh slightly more than their male counterparts. Maybe women are really the ones with the sense of humor! It also may be the reason women live a little longer than men. IJS

> **❝** *You can't be that kid standing at the top of the water slide, overthinking it. You have to go down the chute.* **❞**
> **Tina Fey**

Seven

RELATIONSHIP COMPLICATIONS

I think people attract people based on the baggage that they carry, myself included. Even though I can discuss them today, unfortunately, I did not always know the type of bags I had. Many of us are walking around broken or weak until someone else sees our struggle, or we're put in a situation where we have to acknowledge our bags.

This is never, ever easy. So, brace yourself. One of the most interesting things I've learned is that people can see things in you that you can't see in yourself. So, if you're carrying a sorry ass 'I loved him too long' bag, trust me, somebody sees it! Or, if you're carrying an 'I hate the way I look' bag, trust me, someone can see the fracture in your self-esteem.

The goal is to eliminate those bags, but the only person that can help you eliminate them is you. I believe you have to pray that thing off of you and do the work necessary to become whole.

I pray every day, 'Lord, for every one step I take towards you, please take two steps towards me, I'm not as strong as you!'

Here's something to think about. Life is crazy! It's full of good times, bad times, and even a bunch of non-eventful times, but you have to learn to roll with all the punches. Learn to push forward, even when it seems impossible. I'm one that'll stand back and look at a situation from all angles. How will this affect me? How will it affect the greater community, my family, or my future? Is this a reload of the bags I've already let go of?

I give myself ample opportunity to think through the situations because I don't have the time or the energy for new bags! Another thing to consider when you're letting go of the baggage is to re-evaluate your social circle.

Think about the people you call friends. Are they sowing into you? Are they pulling or pushing you in directions that are unhealthy for your personal growth? Consider this, if you are in a situation where you are always the one giving and people are taking, you have to wonder, 'What am I doing wrong here?'

If you are the victim in every situation, then you gotta figure out, 'Why am I the victim? What am I doing wrong? What energy have I given off?' I'll never forget thinking to myself, "What's the common denominator here?" My answer was always ME!

I asked my friend that same question recently after another unsuccessful online dating saga. I laugh sometimes to avoid crying. I was sharing my story a few nights ago, explaining that a few of my girlfriends and I signed up for online dating. We knew people who had met online and eventually were married, so we thought this could be a good thing.

One of my girlfriends met a guy online. We thought it was great because there was plenty of fish. Or, should I say, sharks! He was a good dude with a nice job and a promising career. Another girlfriend and I thought we could find the same type of man online, but instead of plenty of fish, we got plenty of dicks!

Why in the world were we getting such hits? Were we giving off a vibe that said we need dick? Were we giving off something that said send me pictures of your penis every time you get an opportunity? The craziest thing is that I didn't know they came in so many shapes, colors, and sizes, all over or underdressed, with turtlenecks and hats! LOL!

Confused? You'll get that later! My bio had nothing extra sexy, nothing crazy, especially nothing that says, 'Hey, I'm easy.' To this day, I still don't know. Was it too much leg, too much lipstick? What is it? To say the least, I was turned off.

In a conversation with my friend, I said, "Listen, this online dating has been unsuccessful for me, so I'm going to go ahead and take my conversation back to the good old school ways of meeting people, and I have a source that I believe won't ever fail me." I was not going to be on that website looking for a husband when all I found was a bunch of "I'm not readies." I needed to go back and tell the Man what I needed.

The Man I needed to talk to was God! I had to tell Him what I wanted. I want him to be God-fearing, patient, strong, honest, consistent, and regard me in the highest way possible when he's planning his future. I want my husband to be compassionate to my struggle and understand what I'm going through in this industry. Most importantly, I want my husband to understand what I have been through in my life. I want him to want to protect me and want him to pray for and with me. I'm not saying you can't find that kind of man looking at a picture or two or three bios on Plenty of Fish, but in my case, it was Plenty of Dicks. It just wasn't a success for me!

Who knows why online dating didn't work for me? Maybe I gave off some sort of good guy repellent. Despite the bags I carry, I know what I want now. My ex getting shot caused me to be more transparent with people. I don't have time to play games or play with people's emotions. Based on this, I have some deal-breakers. Things I won't deal with for even one hot second. If I see any of these characteristics in you, I throw up the deuces.

For example, if you can't provide what I need as a man, I will not waste my time with you. I think it's important to say that so everybody is on the same page. I am not being rude or nasty with it, but I do let men know I need them to feed that part of me as a woman. The most important thing for me as a woman is for my man to be a protector and provider. If he can't be those, he has no chance with me.

If he has children, I need to see how he is as a parent. Is he a provider to them? Do they know him and have a relationship with him as their father? I could never be with a man that walks away from his seeds. I don't know everything about everything, but what I do know is that if he won't take care of her children, he won't take care of me or mine. That's a deal-breaker! No ifs, ands, or buts about it.

A man must work! I don't care what he does, he better find a way to hustle up some cash and coins! My love languages are very simple. They are gifts, acts of service, and quality time. You can't do any of those things for KiKi if you don't have a job! I like a man, a real one. I don't care - well, actually I do care - what he does to get those coins, but I should never out-hustle him.

Love Languages

Since I've opened that can of worms, I guess I need to reiterate what I mean by love languages. I read a book named The Five Love Languages by Gary Chapman many years ago and it literally changed how I love. It gave me a better explanation of what I needed as a woman from a man. I learned on a very intricate level how to explain and label my needs to my lover. Per the author, there are five love languages: Quality Time, Acts of Service, Touch, Words of Affirmation, and Gifts. There's way too much to explore but let me give a bird's-eye view of my languages.

Gifts: I'm not saying he must buy me things all the time, or that what he buys has to be expensive or extravagant, but it's important to feel that I'm thought about by my love. I'm sure you're wondering, where the hell did this girl get this from? My father used to always say, "If a man spends his hard-earned money on you, then he's regarding you in a particular way. It's up to you to figure out in which way."

Here's how it works. After a date with me, he learns that I love flowers. Maybe he sends me flowers or even a single rose to let me know I'm on his mind. Maybe he's out of town and he brings me a magnet representing that place, knowing I collect magnets from around the world. These are very simple and fairly reasonable gifts, although a girl could use some new shoes, a car, and oh yeah, a bigger house! Just kidding (actually, I'm not, but you get my drift).

Acts of Service: Service has always had a special place with me. I promise, if I have a man, my car becomes his responsibility. I mean, totally. I shouldn't even have to know where the gas goes.

If he's really about his business, then buying the gas wouldn't be my concern, either. I love a man that shows me he's there for me. It makes me want to be there for him, too. It makes me proud to see him doing those things I can clearly do myself. But why should I, considering that I have him. He feels needed, and it makes him feel appreciated because I am a damsel in distress. A quick way to my heart is to help me do something. Wash my car, trim my trees, paint the house, or help me take my weave out! You may as well call my mama and ask for my hand in marriage because I am done!

Most importantly the key to my heart is quality time. I remember my father telling me, "A man's time is money and his money is his time. A man won't spend time or money on you if he don't want to be bothered." In response to that, my best friend likes to tell me, "Men buy strippers, does that mean he loves her?" My answer is always the same, "No, he bought a service and her time. My man is investing in my well-being and my staying. For all that, I might go ahead and strip for him (wink, wink)."

The Kiana Dancie

When a man wants to spend time, and I mean quality time with me, I'm allowing myself to be open. Quality time for me is everything from intimacy to working out. It's time he could use to do other things with other people, but he chose me and that is the key to my heart.

Am I Asking Too Much?

I tell dudes all the time that if I like you, I am going to sow into you. As your lady, I make the full commitment to helping you become a better you! When, and if, I ever leave you, you'll be a better man. You know there is a level of investment that a woman is supposed to make into a man, the same way a man is supposed to make an investment into a woman. But you have to have your life together. You should be spiritually grounded, financially stable, kind, and consistent in your actions, and should regard me as your lady in our relationship.

I remember I met this guy once, and he did not have a savings account, which is not very uncommon. But he didn't know how to manage money or even have the interest to figure it out. To make matters worse, the man did not even know how to pray, but he was interested in dating me. Ok, you may not know how to pray out loud, but there is no way you can be my man and cannot pray at all. You have to be able to talk to Jesus for you and us!

See, I would be remiss if I didn't remind you that I'm a fussing and cussing comedienne. However, when the chips are down and I'm going through it, I call on Jesus. So, I would deliberately make him pray. When we sat down to eat, I'd bow my head, waiting on his goofy butt to start praying. Even though he would fumble through every word, I would sit there until he said, "Amen."

I was convinced that every time I did this, he would become better. I hoped that one day he would surprise me with a good, church bell-ringing prayer. Clearly, I was disappointed every time. LOL! I eventually told him, "Look you got to get it together. I know the pressure is on you, but you can't be my man because you don't know how to talk to Jesus." Every time we sat down to eat, he went right to his plate.

I was convinced that every time I did this, he would become better. I hoped that one day he would surprise me with a good, church bellringing prayer. Clearly, I was disappointed every time. LOL! I eventually told him, "Look you got to get it together. I know the pressure is on you, but you can't be my man because you don't know how to talk to Jesus." Every time we sat down to eat, he went right to his plate. "You don't know how to talk to God and bless the hands that prepared the food?" He did not know how to thank the Lord, and that was a big deal for me. When I asked him about it, he said, nobody had ever held him accountable.

All I could do was shake my head in disbelief. Nobody ever told him how to pray for himself or his family unit? Even if you're not going to pray for the unit, you should at least be able to pray for the food. I want my man to have an evolving relationship with the Lord. He should be, at the very least, willing, and able to pray so we don't choke on a chicken bone. LOL! I'm laughing, but I'm dead serious. That's a very important attribute a man must-have. I think if a man is serious about a woman, he would pray for her, over her, and yes, with her. Listen, as I tell people all the time, I am fussing and cussing, but I know Jesus, and trust me, He knows me. Don't get it twisted, pooh!

T'at's the S*** I 'on't Like

It may sound strange, but I do not like a guy who is too attractive. That was my ex. After wasting ten good years with him, I wanted the opposite. I prefer the guy who stands in the back of the room and does not need much attention. My theory is YOU cannot be pretty. There is only one 'pretty' in this relationship, and that would be me.

Even though we will complement each other, I don't want my man to be the center of attention. Don't get me wrong, I want my man to be attractive because, clearly, I don't want a dog. LOL! But many of the things that were important then are less important today. See, as an alpha female, I prefer an equal plus. Someone who exudes strength through his actions and focuses less on the way he looks. Someone who is confident, able to carry the load, and is not afraid of a strong female that mirrors him.

I know you are probably wondering, "What is an equal plus?!" Well, an equal plus is someone who is doing a little better than me. If I'm running fast, he's running faster! If I have one brick for the empire, he has two bricks! My experience with very attractive men is that they assume a woman will bow down and allow passes he wouldn't otherwise be afforded. It's my sincere belief that an ugly man loves long and hard! LOL! Don't judge me, learn for yourself!

The same can be said for a man with a lot of money, especially if he's an ugly man. If a man has a lot of money, then you already know he assumes women will fall to his feet, and they usually do. Hence the reason why a former president thought he could just do anything to any woman he desired. For example, grabbing them inappropriately. Those are the thoughts of someone who is nuts, rich, and entitled! It's foolish behavior and in my opinion not the making of a good husband.

Because of my past encounters with men, I guess it's safe to say I have had some trust issues and would carry those issues into new relationships. At times, I carried around what my ex did after catching him in lies and not being where he was supposed to be. He could not keep a job and I tolerated his behavior. He could not take care of me financially or our household.

He couldn't pay bills consistently and yet I was still with him. I won't lie, he tried, but it seemed like he couldn't get his footing. Lord knows, I prayed long and hard for him. I wanted him to be successful, with or without me. It was my most consistent and sincere prayer, "Lord, help this man get his life together!" I learned too many life lessons from my father, and my mother raised me to be a strong woman – I had NO time for this!

Real talk - I can't tell you if that prayer was answered, but I know for sure He heard me pray, "Make me strong enough to get out of anything that binds me!" One day, I walked away from him and all the drama that came with that relationship. There are plenty of women who are with men who aren't about anything and continue to stay because of financial security, or what they perceive as emotional security.

I can't blame them; I stayed too. I can't really pinpoint my reasons, but I stayed. Sometimes for a woman, the financial comfort of a man is the only thing she has. Especially if she has made nothing of her life. Some women think all they have is what's between their legs. She can be dumb as a doorknob but will always be a kept woman.

That was not my life. I had something going on for myself, yet I chose to stay with a man who was trying to better himself but couldn't seem to catch a break. If I had to choose a reason for staying, I'd say it was emotional dependency. He was all I knew forever! I also often think that because he was attractive and set to go pro, I gave him multiple chances. I swear I did. When I wondered why I stayed with him for so long, the answer was that I was so busy looking backward at the time that had been spent instead of looking forward to how much time I'd waste with him in the future.

Everything wasn't all bad, we had some good times as well. I actually have some very fond memories of us together. He always attended my family vacations and reunions. One year, my family and I went to Panama City Beach, FL He didn't go with us because we were fussing and broke up for the one-millionth time. But by the time my family and I arrived at the beach, he was there, claiming he wasn't going to lose me. It was hilarious because he was a very big guy and he drove a tiny car. My mom said, "He drove all the way to the beach in a child-size shoe box to save his girl from the dudes at the beach?" LOL!! We still laugh at this today. My life is hilarious, so I laugh to lighten the load.

Trust Issues

To some degree, I believe we all carry trust issues in every relationship we encounter whether we realize it or not. It's always our experiences that determine our interactions with others. The idea is to never make someone pay for what someone else did to you. Much like going from one job to another, you're going to take experiences from one situation to the next, whether it's positive or negative. It's a choice you have to make to consciously release what has held you mentally hostage. It's a constant battle to decide whether or not I'm going to carry my bags.

Sometimes, I avoided getting into relationships because I didn't want to deal with the drama. I was sure it would be the same stuff, so I just kept it moving, occupying my time with work, being funny, and becoming a better me.

I met a young lady a few months ago, and she referred to me as BAE. I thanked her, then asked her, why she called me BAE? She replied with the proudest response and biggest grin, and said, "Because you're BUILDING AN EMPIRE! I salute you!" That made me smile. It mostly made me proud of myself. As accurate as she was, it reminded me that I am BAE, and I can't stop pushing while I'm waiting on my mister. I have to keep it moving.

Along the way, I had to make some decisions. It was not fair to make my new guy pay for the mistakes that my crazy exes made in the past. However, I will say nine times out of ten, if there are any issues, I can see them coming. Especially now that I am getting older! LOL! I see it all coming.

With that in mind, I'm constantly putting forth the effort to change myself for the better. In doing so, I've stopped dating the same type of dude.

I've allowed myself to be more open-minded, less judgmental, and more understanding of people's situations. Lord, help me! Honey, there are some crazies out there!

See, for me, he doesn't have to be perfect or even have a lot of money, but he must be striving for more. I'm in a place in my life where I want a man with certain things. At the very least, he should have the basics: a place to live, a job, and a car. Dang! Those are what you should have as an adult! Is that too much? LOL! I'm learning that for many, it is too much. What about a savings account, 401 k, and a game plan to take over the world?! Where is the Pinky to my Brain so we can take over the world? My tolerance is very low for men who are not trying to get to the next level. Just as I don't want people playing games with me, I have no time to play with people and their games.

I allow myself to date different men to test the waters, but I am not your mama. I don't have to like or love you. Have your life together enough that somebody would want to stand next to you. I want a man that matches my fly, someone that is motivated by my hustle. He sees me winning and wants to win too, and not be left in my dust. Ironically enough, I always seem to find the same type of dude in a different package. LOL! I guess the saying is true, you like what you like. UGH! I hate dating.

One of the many experiences that makes me feel that way happened with a guy I was seeing. Even though he was not my ideal man, he was very kind, loving, supportive, and TEAM KIANA DANCIE! Y'all know, I love that! I loved that he was very consistent. I don't care what time it was, I knew where he would be every day, either at home or at work. It was simple, but that level of simplicity began to bore me. I would be irritated that he didn't have much going on outside of me. Ugh! All I want is someone in the middle. Someone that has some business about himself and someone who is strong and ready to make me happy. I won't lie, he was hella - yes, I said HELLA - smitten to be with me, but he was way too passive. I felt like it was always a struggle for him to stand up for himself.

I would ask him over and over again, "What do you think? How are you feeling?" His response was always the same, "My opinions don't matter. You're going to do what you want, anyway!" Honestly, he was right, but I valued his opinion and wanted him to man up! I needed a man that would check me when I got out of pocket. Someone that would say, "Lil mama, chill!" But he was meek, very quiet, and always letting things slide to avoid conflict. That would literally run my blood hot! Sometimes you have to confront the issue to get through or past what's going on.

My preference is a man that comes into the room and makes his presence known. Not that he's beating on his chest and hanging from the chandelier, but he's clearly an acknowledged presence in the room. He has an undeniable strength that is assertive, but also skills to communicate about any topic.

I understand that sometimes a man will go to his woman to help make decisions. I expect that, but when a man goes to his woman, he should pretty much have his mind made up of how he would like things to be. To take it further, he may even have an outline of what he needs to do so he can share it with his woman. By doing that, a woman can help her man formulate an entire plan of action. I mean he should at the very least have some ideas of the desired outcome.

The guy I was seeing did not even come to me with any ideas or thoughts for his plans in life. Instead, he was sitting there waiting for me to decide what we were going to do. All the time, every time! All I could say was, "What do you mean what are we going to do?" If I gotta make all the decisions, make all the money, and fight all the battles, why do I need you? Jesus, take this wheel before I run over him!

I Know He Feels Inadequate

I know the bags I carry probably make him feel that way. He says he is doing the best he can, but he needs to make more money. Yes, he does, and I get it. He also needed to stop comparing himself to other guys I have dated or the type of guys he thinks I am used to dating. I'm sure he felt some kind of way, especially when he made comments about the gifts I'd been given or the car I drove. I reminded him not to focus on those things but to focus on what he was able to do and stop comparing himself to other people. I couldn't understand why he was so focused on what someone else did for me.

It was so P-E-T-T-Y! The "I'm not good enough" chord is not sexy! When I'm dating, I can care less about what your ex did for you! That means nothing to me. She's not here anymore. I am! So as far as I am concerned, she was never here, and those things don't matter.

I often wonder why I am single and what, if anything, I am doing wrong? After thinking about it in great detail, I've concluded that it could very well be my bags of lack of trust, being domineering, and being too independent. I honestly think guys are afraid or intimidated by me. Seventy-five percent of the time when men speak to me, it's very passive. It's more of a "Hey, I am testing to see if you reject me before I ask you out." After they say hello, they continue to say things like, "Well, I know you have a man and I have no chance." My answer is always the same, "With that approach, you're right, you don't!"

Men will approach me walking through the door with a defeatist attitude because they have already assumed that I am not available. This puts me in a situation where I have to sell myself like, "Hey brother. How are you doing? I'm God fearing. I don't have any kids. I'm funny, hey, hey, hey! I got my life together and I'm single."

This is ridiculous! I have recently had very candid conversations with my closest single friends, and I find that they, too, are having the same issues. This is not only crazy but sad. All I can ask is, 'What are we going to do?' My answer to that question is always the same -- keep pushing!

However, I am so over jumping through hoops trying to prove I am really single and open to having a Mister. You'll never hear or see me try to convince nobody's son I am worthy of his time! Guys do not believe a woman like me, who is in front of crowds entertaining people, fairly attractive in her own right, is all the 'wells' and has it all together is single. Why wouldn't somebody snatch her up?

Now, I am not saying I haven't had opportunities, but I do not want to pick up anybody that has baggage that is heavier than mine. I'm definitely not going to dim my light for him, so he'll be running himself in circles trying to figure me out. I am not going to do it, so if you don't have your life together, we can't be together. Find another target, sir!

What I need in my life is somebody who is solid, someone that is a team player and is clear on his position in my life. I want someone that has a clear picture of his future. If you do not have a clear idea of what you want your life to be, then there is nothing we can discuss. I need a man I can look to for direction. A man I can look to for advice that he doesn't pull out of his ass. If you do not have that, then what can you do for me? What can we do for each other for that matter? I have released a lot of my baggage and have overcome many of my various trust issues, so why would I connect with someone that is still in the midst of their struggle?

I will be the first to admit that sometimes people just need a hand-up, so I won't completely shut you down. But I do give them enough rope to see if they'll hang themselves. The goal is to make sure I am using my discernment to try to keep good people around me. The reality is that sometimes you just don't know. To be honest, I think I'll always have a sense of 'I don't know them, and I don't know their people!' So, when I deal with them, it's with precaution. There will always be a little of that in me, but I do what I can to not be a pessimist. I've been told many times that I don't appear to want a family. I am not sure what that look is that I give off to others. I do make it very clear I am not hunting down a man, but I do desire children and a
husband.

I told my mother the other day, "I don't know when it's going to happen, or if it's ever going to happen, so be patient! If all else fails, I guess you and I will be two old ladies with dogs sitting on the couch!" She rebukes this statement frantically.

Studies show that while individuals usually rank "appearance" as very high on their list when looking for a mate, we tend to find individuals who laugh more attractive.

> **But only in their dreams can men be truly free. It was always thus and always thus will be.**
> **Robin Williams**

Eight

BAGGAGE REMOVAL

For years I had bags under my eyes that altered my appearance and made me look like I was always tired. I remove decided to have Blepharoplasty, a big word for a small surgery, which is the official name of the procedure to them. It was painful, but it was worth it! After the surgery, I looked younger and more refreshed. I am in a competitive business where I have to put my best face forward - LITERALLY! Every time I go to work, I need to make sure I feel good about myself because when people look at me as a stand-up comedienne, they may make a lot of assumptions.

No one has ever accused a stand-up comedian of being too ugly, but I'm also an actress. When an opportunity comes around, I want the powers that be to say, "She's pretty, she's funny, and she's talented! She's a triple threat."

I'm in a crazy industry dominated by men. It's their world and they will quickly tell a female the only way you can get ahead is if you screw yourself to the top, or to the middle, lol! Trust me, there are a lot of ladies that thought they were making the right decision to sleep with someone, believing it would help them get to the next level. After she gave up the goods, she lost her leverage. He can now help her or drop her. Either way, she risks losing her ass, literally!

I have learned that baggage can come from multiple sources. Some of it you recognize, while others you may not until it has weighed you down, slowed your run to a walk, and then eventually put you on your knees. Just because I'm carrying the bags does not mean I packed them. It just means that at some point on my journey, I accepted some of this junk as my own. Sometimes we intentionally refuse to talk about it, refuse to let it go, or just refuse to acknowledge that something is wrong and needs to be addressed. We have to acknowledge it, address it, then release it.

The airport is a perfect place to analyze your bags. When you first get to the baggage check they ask you very specific questions: Are these your bags? Did you personally pack your bags? Did anyone ask you to carry a bag for them?

The gate agent gives you one chance to declare your baggage by giving you a claim check to pick up your bags once they have been taken off the plane. Just like most things in life, you have a choice. After exiting the plane, you can pick up your bags at baggage claim, or you can leave them. It's a decision you are free to make. Some of us pick them up when we really should let them stay where they are, but we've been so used to carrying them with such an emotional attachment, we feel that we have to pick them up. Trust me, you are not your bags, no matter how heavy, light, deep, dark, old, fancy, shabby, or scary. They may be your bags, but your bags don't and shouldn't define you. The baggage we carry might even belong to someone else. We often ignore the signs to recognize that we're carrying someone else's bags.

For example, your father was a dark-skinned man who cheated on and left your mama. Now you might hate dark-skinned men based on how your mama was treated by one. More specifically, you have daddy issues because your father left your mother, and you perceived it as he left you! Every situation is VERY different but when everything is sorted out, you may find out he tried to connect with you, but you were so closed off or overly protected by your hurt mother that the connection was never an option. So be careful and very aware of the baggage you carry. Did you pick it up intentionally? Were they given to you? All I'm saying is that it's easy to confuse someone else's baggage with your own.

I have always had to compartmentalize people to make relationships work and I believe many people do the same thing. Yes, we're friends. Yes, I know you. Yes, I like you. You are good enough for me to speak to and break bread with, but you may not be good enough to come into my home, be associated with or meet my mama. You may be good people, but not the right fit for my brand.

Honey, I just pray about it and pay close attention to who and what I put in my personal space. I also say, people know me, but they don't truly know me.

It's interesting that one of my dearest friends, Rodney Perry, a fellow comedian always tells me, "Kiana, you operate like you're on your own island!" My response is always the same, "Wait till I own one!" I'm just doing me.

See, what I have learned as I've gotten older is that people will call you and want to unload all of their crap on you and you have to say, "Wait a minute, I didn't ask for all this. So, take it back!"

I'm telling you - you have to be clear in order to protect yourself and yours! You can never let people drop their baggage on you. They will feel better, and you will feel horrible because they gave you all their stuff. I'm older and much wiser now. I can hear it from the first word out of their mouth and from that first word, I'm like, "Hey, let me call you back!" I don't want NO parts of that drama, suga! I don't want this to be misinterpreted as I can't lend an ear to a friend in need, but it's a time and place for all things! If your bags are almost running over with your own drama don't allow anyone to dump more on you!

Beware of Baggage Belonging to You

Looking back at my life, I've learned that it really does matter where you drop those bags off. It's important that you stay conscious of your pickups and drop-offs. If you're not careful, you might think you are dropping your bags off along with all your drama. But in reality, you're picking up someone else's. My conversations with my girlfriends are hilarious and I always start with, "I need your ear." Those words give my friends an opportunity to accept or decline to view the contents of the baggage I am preparing to share, or really exchange, with them. It's rare that girlfriends talk and sip tea (i.e., be messy) without exchanging a little baggage. The first thing they should say is, "Girl, I got you. What's going on!" If it's not a good time for them, you'll be warned immediately!

You never want to voluntarily drop off your unsolicited or unwanted bags to your family and friends. They are allowing you to open your bags to share the contents, not take them as their own. You are giving them a fair warning and they can decide.

I'm careful about the people I lend my ear to. I never want to lend my ear to someone I know who carries toxic baggage. Then I'll be sick and frustrated trying to figure out their baggage all while struggling with my own!

I can recognize some of the things people have been through, especially when we start speaking. Being that I am in full control of my world, I decide if I'm going to allow people to unload those bags on me. Knowing what I've been through, it's my choice. I have a gift because I've been through it, but don't take my gifts for granted, EVER!

I cannot undo what I have been through, but I can do all I can to NOT reload my bags. I work daily to keep my universe positive and drama-free. I go to war for those that I love, and I do all I can to move forward, bagless. But, just like anything, you have to make a conscious effort to let it all go.

I'm the first to say I love you, but you cannot unload your bags on me. Nothing good will come if you keep holding on to what happened to you. Let it all go! You know it's going to be a situation where you talk to somebody and they are going to tell your business, but that is something I have never cared about because I don't have any stories that I'm ashamed of. When I tell you something about me, first, remember I was the one who told you. That means I promise you it's the way I wanted you to know it. So, if I hear something about me in the streets and it's wrong, I'm going to say, "You know what, let me correct you because I own all my own stuff."

You do not have to tell anybody your business. You do not have to unload your bags. You do not have to tell anybody what you've been through, or what you are going through. But if you choose, you do have the ability to tell people your story. Remember, if it came from you, then it's all your truth!

Make sure you tell the story the way you want it to be told. So that when it comes full circle, you can own it! You can acknowledge it and recognize, "Hey, that's my story." Then ask yourself:

Did I learn from it?
What lessons did I learn from it?

Did I get something positive from my story?
Have I let all the hurt from this situation go?

I Have Done Nothing Wrong and If I Did Do
Something Wrong, I Own That Too.

You know how you may wear a piece of jewelry in the sun you may not have really liked the piece, but it matched your outfit, so you tolerated it? You just didn't want to look plain. You were out in the sun, hanging out, and frolicking. Now the sun has made an impression on your chest that outlines this average piece of jewelry, whether you love it or not. Did you really need it to make your outfit complete at the expense of making a mark on yourself that would last way beyond you taking off the outfit?

Now it's a part of you for an unknown period of time. Although it's not a permanent mark and will eventually go away, you have to deal with it and adjust, so you do not look crazy.

That piece of jewelry is similar to the bags we carry. I have definitely carried some bags a bit too long and they have made marks on me that have changed the way I look at myself, people, places, and even things surrounding me. They have also changed the way I interact with people or with life in general.

The marks may have changed my perception of life, but through effort, prayer, and time, as time heals all wounds, they will go away. During the time I was trying to allow myself to heal, I may have missed opportunities, people, or other things because I was so focused on the mark that I missed the moment. I may have done or not done certain things because I was ashamed of the mark or felt I needed to hide it. These marks are the baggage that keeps us stuck or reacting in a way we should not have reacted had we not had that mark on us.

I'm mad I have a blemish on my skin, and I do not want to walk around with this scar on me. Every day, I'm rubbing Scar Be Gone ointment, vitamin E, grape seed oil, and all kinds of oils to get rid of this scar. I'm mad because I messed up my skin. I don't want to walk around and explain to people why it's there, what happened or deal with people asking if my boyfriend cut me. Now I have to explain how I got this scar on my body. It's ugly and unattractive. The story might be funny, and the story might be sad, but at the end of the day, I must decide what I will share or not if somebody asks.

You Attract What You're Carrying

You have to put some nice things in your bag instead of carrying around your rotten meat from past relationships. Learn how to lighten your load. Maybe you can put soothing songs, gifts, healthy fruits, great experiences, beautiful stories, positive relationships, and opportunities that you would never have encountered if you had not allowed certain things to happen. You must understand that you receive what you open yourself up to receive. If you focus on those things that open yourself and allow someone to pray for you and the situation you're dealing with, it may help you attract better things because you're carrying better stuff.

Just because you look good, smell good, and have your head high and shoulders back does not mean you have it all together. This is a trick of the baggage carrier. Even though you are carrying baggage, it does not mean you are supposed to walk with your back hunched over, head hung down low, crying, with your makeup running and your hair looking a mess.

I remember my grandfather telling my mother, 'You are cut from the Dancie cloth, you never walk around looking like what you've been through.' Now my mother tells my brother and I that same thing, 'You don't have to look like you've been or are going through something. We have all been through something, but you are cut from the Dancie cloth and that's what we don't do. Pull your head up, arch your back, straighten your crown and put a smile on your face.'

Studies show that even when you're not feeling like you want to smile, a smile makes you feel better. It is something about those hormones and electrolytes. Something goes on in your body when you smile. It makes you feel better, and it makes people around you act better. They cannot help it.

It is up to you to decide what you need to carry on your journey. Sometimes you just have to rearrange your bags, but sometimes you have to lighten the load by letting go of some stuff.

I had to realize that I had compartmentalized my baggage, so they had been allocated to different areas based on my needs and expectations. From a woman, sister, daughter, friend, and at one time somebody's prospective girlfriend's perspective, I had to rearrange my bags to make sure I was not allowing them to interfere with any of the roles I am expected to play. Through my experiences, I have gained strength, wisdom, and power, and I carry these things in my bags as well. It's important not to unload those things that help you stay focused and live your best life.

The rearrangement of my bags was necessary because if I walked around with that scar of child molestation heavy on my heart, it would be heavy on my mother's heart. If she knew or thought, I was walking around still affected by that experience, she would be affected by it as well. As a family, we went through it. As a family, we decided not to stay in it. I went through therapy as a young girl. My mother made sure that I had the opportunity to talk about my challenges as much as possible. I believe therapy is something that should be a very viable option.

Black people rarely go to a therapist to talk about things that are going wrong or to talk about the trauma they suffered because the response is often, "You just need prayer," or, "Just let that go. Get over it." Sweeping stuff under a rug is like putting a band-aid on a gaping wound and expecting it to stop the bleeding. I tried that when I literally almost cut my finger off, slicing chicken. It took my brother to force my mom to take me to urgent care. Eight stitches and a tetanus shot later; I learned that the band-aid would have NEVER worked.

Sometimes you need to talk to somebody who's been through a similar experience and can help you shift your perspective. Seeing it from another angle helps. Sometimes your answer from Christ will not come immediately, so in the meantime, you may need to talk to someone that can help you process your thoughts to get through it and this person is trained to do just that. Ideally, the professional you speak with is trying to help you sort through your mess. Christ may even use them to help you. See, my mess is my mess, your mess is your mess. If we get two messy people together, baby, that is a problem.

A therapist is trained, and they will not lie to you. I was blessed because one of my friend's mom, Karen, was a psychiatrist. She would sit and talk to me and my best friend for hours. Our little sessions were probably why I turned out to be alright. I grew up with a psychiatrist, and no, she did not write me any prescriptions, although she probably needed to. It was a blessing to have that woman say, "Go sit on the couch."

I learned that expressing myself was very therapeutic and made my baggage seem much lighter than it had been in the past. Therapy was great for me. I believe there are a lot of people that need therapy and they just don't get it. Yes, I had emotional baggage, but at least it was cute and it matched. Let me be very clear, God covers me with His feathers; and I find refuge under His wings, (Psalm 91:4).

We all compare our bags because we want to know if we are the only ones going through this thing. You know how you go out with your girlfriends and get yourself a glass of wine or whatever it is that you do to unload? As soon as you say, "Girl, let me tell you what happened!" Before you know it, you're comparing bags. This can only be done with true friends. You may really go through it and struggle to carry all your bags. Once you unload your bags, you feel lighter and realize it is a blessing to do that with friends. What usually happens is once you unload your bags, you listen to them unload and you say, "Lord, my bags ain't that heavy." The spirit of gratitude makes you appreciate your situation better when you look at what you're going through in relation to other people's situations. This may sound unfortunate or selfish but I'm like, "Man, I wish that is all I had to deal with." Or "Thank God that is all I had to deal with."

The average person laughs around 13 times a day. Oddly enough, very few of those times are due to a joke or an intentional action. More often, we laugh at chance happenings or things that were never intended to be funny in the first place.

The Kiana Dancie

BEFORE SURGERY

AFTER SURGERY

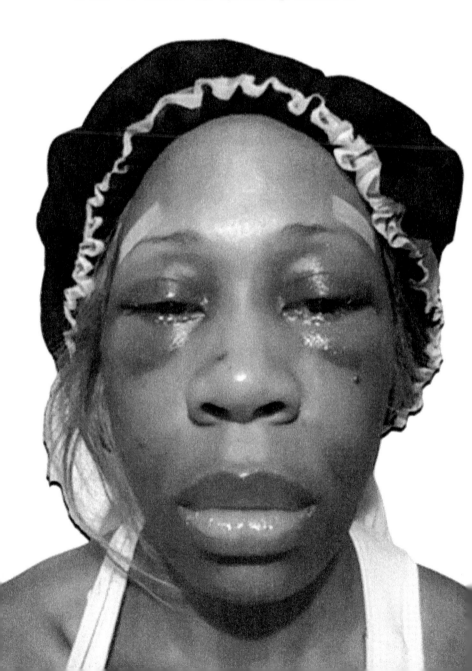

The Kiana Dancie

> **❝** *I used my imagination to make the grass whatever color I wanted it to be.* **❞**
>
> **Whoopi Goldberg**

Nine

THE GRASS AIN'T GREENER

I have one good girlfriend. I won't mention her name just in case she reads my mook. She comes from a strong, united family. When she got married, she had a huge wedding. When I tell you this girl had 14 bridesmaids in her wedding, I'm not exaggerating. She had so much money given to her that I could not believe my eyes. She's African and she explained that is a tradition at weddings. Her friends and family sprayed her with money, (by the way I loved this!). In Black American culture, we call this "making it rain!" She had so much money, they hired an armed guard to protect them as they took the money out. She and her husband walked away with about $50,000 that night, if not more. I thought to myself, 'Wow, they look so happy.' People traveled from all over the world to see her and celebrate her special day.

Her mother was an African princess. Of course, that means nothing to us Black Americans, but to them, it's definitely a big deal. She showed me articles and news stories from back home that read, 'The Princess' Daughter is Getting Married!' Her family threw her this big ceremony! Oh my God, it was beautiful! It kind of made me jealous and maybe even a little sad. I was just a Black American girl, minus the traditions of my ancestors.

They have been married since 2007, but I got wind that something was going on. I reached out and said, "Baby girl, what's going on with you?" She explained that she wanted to get away, so she drove over an hour away to sit and spill all the juice! I can remember thinking, "Girl, what's wrong with you?! It must be serious because that's a long drive." When she saw me, she burst into tears and said, "He's having a baby with the neighbor!" My only response was, "WAIT WHAT? Who's having a baby with the neighbor? YOUR HUSBAND!?"

I couldn't believe it! I can't even begin to imagine what she felt like. Now, don't get me wrong, I have been cheated on, but I have NEVER had to deal with a baby on the way. Even in my ten-year relationship – the kids came before we got together. Not only did she feel betrayed and cheated, but to add insult to injury, she was going to see this chic carrying her man's child, and of course, he was going to raise it! She and her husband already had a child, and that had been a struggle. They had multiple miscarriages before the birth of their first and only son.

She wanted to have another kid, but they were having a hard time, so he said, "Since you were having a hard time giving me another baby, I thought I would get one with somebody else, and I thought you would be happy." REALLY! This dude was dead serious! Since that day, my respect for her has grown. I don't know if I could have dealt with that, nor do I think I would have stayed with him.

All this time, since her wedding, I was always thinking she was living in wedded bliss and getting everything she wanted. She wore all the name-brand designers and had a huge house and a brand-new car. From the outside looking in, the picture looked great. It looked like a picture I envisioned for my life. Funny how things really are once the layers are peeled back. I did not understand the cost she was paying to have that life and how it affected her. I had no idea what she was going through, and I felt immensely close to her after she opened up to me about her most personal issues and the sacrifices that she made for her son. She demonstrated great strength and resilience in her circumstance, and her sacrifice as a mother is unmatched.

Many people may not understand why a woman stays with a man who cheats, and for you, it may very well be one of your dealbreakers. However, you will never know how you will respond until you are in the same situation. I know for me it was never anything I saw for myself. Even though it may appear I was with my ex for the full ten years, when a situation would happen, we broke up for months at a time until finally, I left for good.

Here I am thinking about how lucky she is and how much better her life is because of the picture I perceived to be true. But in reality, she was miserable and suffering from her own baggage. I was so busy comparing my bags to hers that I overlooked that my friend was hurting. My bags did not have a husband, a child, or a big house! Ironically, my bags had the desire to have the things she had in her life before I never really knew what price she was paying for those things. I was comparing my single life to her perfect 'picket fence and married' life. Well, can you guess what she was doing? Comparing her own life to mine.

As we sat there, my friend said something I would never have thought I would hear her say, "Kiana, I wish I could travel like you." Here I am thinking I just want to be able to sit at home and relax, cook for my man, raise my kids, and yes, pick drapes for the dining room. Of course, this was not my life. It was hers! LOL!

The beautiful, yet ugliest thing about my life is that I don't have a 9-5 job. As a professional entertainer money is sometimes short or plentiful. My personal life suffers due to me always being on the road, but the perception from others is that I live a good life void of absolutely ANY worries! All people see is that I dress nice, have a nice home, drive a beautiful car, keep my hair and nails done and face beat, and rarely do people see me wear anything twice. It might be easy to think I have it all together when really, I am just trying to figure it out.

I was looking at my life all wrong comparing apples to oranges and thinking the grass was greener on the other side. I had not realized that it was an illusion and actually the grass over there was dying. The truth is, I am a single woman. I can kick it when I want, go as I please. I'm here. I'm there. And I have friends who love me. My friends support me because they know I am a winner, and my dream is attainable.

I often hear my friends say, "Kiana, you're always traveling, you're always with your famous friends." What they don't know about is my multiple struggles. They don't know that when I sit still, it costs me! When my feet aren't moving, the cash doesn't grow! They do not know I am banking on shows I haven't even received deposits for yet and I'm counting the money I do not have yet. They do not know I have dreams so big that they scare me. They don't know I have dreams to take care of my mother that have not been realized yet.

I want my mother to sit back and relax! I do not want her to work. I don't want her to worry about working another day in her life. I want her to do what she wants to do. If she wants to pick up and go to Vegas for a week or a month, I want her to do that. They do not know the cost I am paying to chase my passion and have a career in entertainment. They do not know I often think that cost is a husband, a child, and a family. They just think my life is glamorous. Although it is (LOL), it didn't happen without me paying a pretty penny! I mean a brand new, shiny, pretty penny!

My mother says all the time, "Your dream is your wish list to God." Make your dreams as big and as crazy as your mind might imagine, and then go to work and watch God make your dreams come true. I've always believed that to be true; the Lord knows my heart. He even knows my deepest desires and He won't ever leave me.

We all have issues and situations. The thing to remember is to run your own race and not compete against or measure yourself by someone else's perceived success. You never know what someone else has risked or sacrificed to get to where they are or gain the things they have.

My Baggage Doesn't Define Me

My baggage might give you a little insight into who I am, but it doesn't give you the full picture. We often look at people and think they have it all together, but we only see what they want us to see. There are days when I feel like my baggage is light, on others feel weak. Some days it feels so heavy that I cannot keep carrying it. Other days, I feel like I do not have the strength or the power to keep pushing. I do so much for so many people that depend on me, and that adds to my baggage even though I accept the responsibility to carry it. Many of us are going through some of the same things. I am coming into my late thirties, not married, with no children, but at the end of the day, I decide and choose what I wanted to do today.

I am in the entertainment business; a business designed to destroy me and break me down. Nothing I do is right and nothing I do is good enough, but I have to make decisions that are best for me daily. I decide whether I'm going to stay in this game to live my dream or not. I ask myself, "Am I in this game to win, or am I in this business to fail and allow everyone to tell me I'm not good enough or funny enough to succeed?"

Retaliation Sac

Now and then, I wonder about the person who shot my high school love. Are his people 'looking' for me? I'm a public figure and easy to find. His killer was up for parole a few years ago, and I wrote a letter in hopes the prison review board would deny his request. I struggled with that because I was thinking to myself, first of all, when he did this, he was a young man and we all make mistakes. Maybe not as detrimental or fatal, but we make them.

I hope he spent his time in jail learning from those mistakes and working to become a different person. Because I still love my high school boyfriend so much, I am still bothered that he is not here. I do not want his murderer to get out of jail and then enjoy his life, because my high school love does not have that ability. I have forgiven him because if I don't, I have empowered him. The last thing I want to do is give him any power. I do not think he meant to kill my boyfriend. He was young, dumb, intimidated, and challenged. He felt like he had something to prove, but do I really care about that right now? All of this is what I continue to tell myself, but I still carry the baggage of fear - Fear that I may run into him or his family one day and the outcome will not be in my favor.

I do not have a clue what his family looks like. I did not know him that well, so his family could have been at one of my shows and I would have no idea. His people don't know my high school boyfriend's - family, they know me, and if they are holding onto the association, the anger, and the resentment towards me and my boyfriend's family, that could be a problem.

I may look over my shoulder wondering if today is the day that someone will come to me and say, "Hey, I'm Charles' people, and you put him in jail." I don't think about it every day and it's actually rare that I do. Lately, it has come across my mind because I'm on TV again. I've become a public figure and I have moved back to Atlanta. All I can do is keep it moving and stay prayed up, so I know I'm covered. All I did was tell the truth.

I did not pull the trigger, so he has to pay the consequences. He committed the crime and that's the reality of what happened. I do not think he meant to kill my boyfriend, but he did it. We all do a lot of things we don't mean to do, but we have to face the consequences and pay for our mistakes. Therefore, this is a sac I'm still working to unpack. I remind myself that I am more than a conqueror. Romans 5:31 says – If God is for us, who can be against us? I won't spend another day worrying about the enemy. PERIOD!!

Fueled by Fear

I feared not being successful and starting something, I can't figure out how to finish. I feared never being married. I feared not meeting the right guy. I feared

not becoming a mother. I feared not making my mother a grandmother. Or not making my brother and uncle.

Even if I wanted to go back to Corporate America, I would have to explain this whole situation, and start back at the bottom, because it has been so long. When things got tight a few years ago, I tried to get a job. Before I even got in the door, they were Googling me and looking at my website. I got the job and managed a team, but it was hard for them to take me seriously.

Sure, I tell jokes, but today we are in the boardroom, and I have to convince people ain't nothing funny about me coming to fire you! Especially since I've worked so hard to get them to take me seriously. Mind you, I really didn't want to be there, I was just there for the check. My body and mind were there temporarily, but my heart was not there at all.

So now I'm in this thing, and I have to figure out how I'm going to stay. I was determined to sustain myself. There are so many people who look like they have it going on, but they don't have a pot to piss in. They're not eating, and I never wanted to be one of those people.

I also feared failure. I feared not leaving a legacy. I feared because my mother is getting older and there is a lot of responsibility on me. I can't even begin to explain. I don't even feel right leaving my mother to tour. It is not fair for my brother to come live with her when he has not even started his life good. I feared not being in the right place if something were to happen to my mother. I feared not being able to take care of her.

Fear has been my motivation. It was my water, my fuel, my oil. Fear kept my joints moving. It kept my engine running. I cannot give up. There is no looking back. I can't go back to Corporate America because they don't want me, and I don't want them. After getting closer to Christ, I refused to let fear hold me hostage. 2 Timothy 1:7 says, For God has not given us a spirit of fear and timidity, but of power, love, and self-discipline. When I don't know anything else to say, I recite the word. I will always be covered! I am the daughter of the King.

Affirming Me

I practice telling myself I am who I am, so I do not regret any of my decisions. I accept that I made them and am okay with who I am, so, to hell with you if you are not. I'm not living my life for anyone else's pleasure or approval. I am living my life because this is me, and God and my family are all I have.

We all have a very short time on this earth, and the goal should be to maximize our opportunities, leave a positive impact on people, and bring joy to as many people as possible. Although I work a lot, I try to sleep until my eyeballs open each day. If I have nowhere to go, I am not going to rush myself. If I only have a few things to take care of, I'm going to take my time and do them. I sleep as much as I can because I want to relax, and I want to look good. I carried enough baggage under my eyes for years, so I make a point to take it easy whenever I can.

Every day, I wake up and remind myself that I can do whatever I choose to do and be whomever I want to be. I never allowed my baggage to weigh me down to where I stopped or gave up. Although it gets heavy at times, I never use the words can't or won't. Instead, I use the words I will, and I can. I use words of affirmation to make me feel like nothing is impossible for me to accomplish. When people tell me no, I say you couldn't be talking to me because no is not an option or a word I understand. If someone tells me no, I am going to find somebody else who will give me that yes. Yes, is a word that I FULLY understand and appreciate!

We all have baggage in some form or another, and odds are when you get rid of some of your bags, others will appear. The key is to know how to eliminate what is unnecessary and use the baggage you have to carry the things that may be beneficial later. I'm focused on my career and my goals. I want to build a production company, write more books, and produce movies. I want people to scream my name from the back of the theater. I want you to know who I am when I walk into the room, so there is no reason to ask, 'Who is she?'

I want my reputation to speak so loudly, that I do not have to introduce myself. I have bills to pay, mouths to feed and at some point, I want to relax. I have nothing to prove to anybody but myself. I want to enjoy my life and that does not mean working my heels off until the end. Life is to be enjoyed and I am vowing to allow a small space for my baggage that fuels me and lose the baggage that brings no benefit. I have my game plan together, which includes having children and a husband who loves me unconditionally, even though I may have a few conditions for him (I'm just saying). Although I don't have a man now, and I am definitely not pregnant yet, I have things I'm trying to accomplish. I want to be comfortable, but I also want to leave a legacy. I want to feed my family through my efforts.

Anytime I laugh at my bags or make someone laugh at their own, I feel good. We often take ourselves and our situations too seriously. So, if I can get you to put your bags down, if not permanently, then maybe just for a few moments to rest and regroup, I have accomplished something.

One bag I already feel like I have loosened is feeling like I haven't made it yet or that I don't deserve to be here. In my mind, I have arrived. Everything I accomplish from this point on is just one more layer of what I'm already doing on my journey to the top. My future is filled with hope and prosperity. God's hand is all over me and my future.

"For I know the plans I have for you," declares the Lord, "plans to prosper you and not to harm you, plans to give you hope and a future."
- Jeremiah 29:11

In studies that looked at laughter in adults versus children, it was found that kids tend to laugh about three times more than adults. Think like a kid and learn to enjoy yourself a little!

> **66** *May I never forget, on my best day, that I need God as desperately as I did on my worst day.* **99**
> **Mike Epps**

Ten

SISTER CIRCLE

I hesitated writing this for literally two hesitated years. I have many reasons for doing so, but the main reason is because I didn't know where to start and I didn't want to relive it again. So, here I am, reliving it

I had reached a point in my life and career where Atlanta was no longer it for me. I thought about LA. because I had lived there multiple times before. Every time I left LA. I came back to Atlanta. I stuck with LA. but LA. didn't stick with me. As you can see, this is where the conflict came in. However, I reached the point of making a final decision on where I would live and advance my career. Only this time, I decided I would no longer use Atlanta as a fallback plan. After much thought and consideration, I finally made my decision. LA. is where I would land again.

Moving is a lot of work but moving to another coast is a whole different process, and I didn't have a plan. What I knew is that in order for individuals to make it in the entertainment industry, they had to be in New York, Atlanta, or LA. However, I never stopped working. I had been a regular guest, twice a month, on a locally produced show in Atlanta, ATL & CO. I have never been one to have a shortage of opinions or thoughts and that is what would happen whenever I appeared. I was having a good time, but this was not enough to keep me in Atlanta. So, I continued making moving arrangements.

On the day that I scheduled a transportation company to pick up my vehicle and was supposed to board my final flight to LA, I received a call from a gentleman who was a producer of Atlanta and Company. I now see the irony of this moment. I thought the call was random. He and I had talked in the past, but it had been a while and this call seemed to have come out of the blue. I answered the phone, and he began telling me about this opportunity to be cast on an upcoming show. He had no details other than it was a talk show with an all-black woman cast shot here in Atlanta. They were looking for Black women with BIG personalities and lots of opinions. As he started going down the list of requirements - I kept saying, "That's me!" "I'm her!" "You know it!" "Let's go!"

As we were talking, I reminded him that I was in the middle of moving to LA. He stressed repeatedly that I should give this serious consideration for a number of reasons, but predominantly because I fit the description of what the network was looking for. Almost to the point where I questioned, "Do I have the damn job or not?" LOL.

The show was to have a "panel" feel, where each host would share their thoughts and opinions, as well as interview celebrities and people from the community. This was very much a black version of "The View." He knew that I would be perfect. And so, did I.

I hesitated because my plan was to be gone. I didn't want to audition for anything in Atlanta because I wasn't going to be there anymore. And yet, something told me to say yes, so I did. I made some phone calls to the transportation company to change the day that they were picking up my truck and then I made the dreaded phone call to the airline company. If you have flown anywhere in the world, you know how difficult it is to get a flight changed. Many airlines refuse to do it and those that will allow it, don't do so without accessing the appropriate fees.

This must have been God's grace because I had no problems with either company. I was able to change my flight with no problems or penalties. After rearranging my schedule, I gave the producer of the show a call. I told him that I had changed my plans per his urging and now I am ready. I had finally changed my plans, but I also wanted him to understand that I wasn't doing this for no reason. It was for this job that he just knew I was a good fit. I put all my reservations to rest.

The next day I received a phone call from the actual show's producer. She gave me more details about the show and asked me if I would come in for a meeting with her. Hearing this additional detail from someone who actually worked on the show helped to also alleviate my fears. We scheduled the meeting within the week. During that time, I was researching talk shows. I was looking online to find any information and details about the show. I even tried reaching out to people who were connected in that circle. My goal was to get as much information about the show as possible as this was very hush-hush. I couldn't find anything online or in my conversations with people that were outside of what I had already been told.

While I was waiting, it seemed like the day of the meeting took forever to arrive. On the day of our scheduled meeting, it was a phone conversation. We talked about my family history and background. During that phone call, I discovered the details of my life were very different from the rest of the potential cast mates. I was the only single woman, who grew up in a single-woman-headed household, with no children - for example. She really wanted to get a feel for who I was as a person. We talked at length and at the end of the phone call, I felt extremely confident that this conversation would land me an opportunity to be considered as a cast member of the show.

She then asked to see me in person. Before I could give her the details, I participated in a chemistry test. For those who are unfamiliar, a chemistry is along the lines of a mock show. It was grueling. We sat with every cast member, ten girls in total. There may have been more because there were only four seats. There was no real formula to this, I thought. A lot of uncertainty surrounded this chemistry test. They were very elusive with the details. On that day, she sat us with two people, then one person, then three people, and the next time four. It became evident that she preferred four people, for this was the format she kept going back to. This is when we understood what she was going for. Some of the people who auditioned had an amazing following, but they could not pass the on-screen chemistry test.

Others had no personality at all. Then it got to the point where our chemistry was flawless.

We looked at each other and we just knew. To be honest, it wasn't clear if the producers felt the same way we did. After we finished our chemistry test - the final four - we went out for dinner and drinks. We made our own decision that we would be the cast. We made our pact that evening. It was so crazy; it was almost magical. I only knew one of the cast members and none of them really knew me. In the back of my mind, I always questioned if they wondered how I got there? Or if I belonged? In their minds, I had not ever been on a television show of their caliber. This was never expressed verbally, but it showed up in their actions.

We went back and met with the producer and shared with her our pact. She agreed and we were the four cast members of Sister Circle Live. The very first day on set, we were all there playing in makeup - and doing our thing. I'm remembering a specific situation involving a makeup artist. I went in with the attitude that maybe the makeup artist was going to use me as his model. Unbeknownst to me, one of the cast members had already arranged for him to do it to her liking. She made a big deal about how my hair should be styled and what my eyeshadow should be. I went along with it because I wanted to play nice and also leverage a relationship with my new sisters. I literally hated my makeup and decided from that day forth to continue to speak up about anything that I didn't like.

Out of her mouth, she said, "I'm ready to introduce the new Kiana." I was totally thrown by this statement. Although they may have thought I was not on "their level," I was still my own person, and no one was going to make me do anything I was not comfortable with. And I still thought I was the baddest in the room. I felt like I was Cinderella, and they were my stepsisters. Someone was always straightening my hair, commenting about my clothes, and always auto-correcting me when I say something, whether it was wrong, funny, or correct. One of them always had something to say. I learned to use my comedic skills and just laugh it off or make a joke. Many times, during interviews, I have been asked "Were you the class clown in school?" Ironically, I was never the clown, but I was crowned Drama Queen in High School. I never had to use my comedic skills to deter bullies or even to get through my day-to-day life. Becoming a cast member on Sister Circle Live, that was the EXACT reason I was chosen, using my comedic skills not only daily, but literally every minute. I was the pretty funny chic on the show, and I made sure to do my part every day. Going to work every day was like working on my stand-up comedy special; One me. One mic. JestHer.

Being a member of an ensemble cast, I never forgot that as a comedian you are onstage alone. I was very comfortable with being on the outside and not being included in their inside jokes and lunches. This conflict went on all the time, between me, my co-hosts, and the makeup artists. Every day, I had no idea what I was walking into. I often talked to my stylist, and she would say, "I can't believe you didn't see the shade they threw." My response was that I didn't have to fight every battle or attend every party I am invited to. There was a lot of shade in and out of the green room, but because I represent the light of Christ; I shine wherever I go, (Matthew 5:13-16).

One day, I remember walking in to get my makeup done and a new makeup artist was there. The head makeup artist told me that this artist was doing my makeup and not my regular artist. When I asked why I was told because he was the boss, and he could make any adjustments that he chose to. I quickly reminded him that I was one of the co-stars and he may be the boss of the artists, but not of my face and whom I worked with. That was my choice, and I was going to be working with whomever I chose. He was very adamant about how my makeup should be, down to the eyeliner on my bottom lid, which he knew that I didn't like. There were many incidents like this.

Yes, we were arguing over eyeliner. It was extremely petty, but it also described the daily environment as I walked into on set. We had multiple disagreements over a lot of petty queen things, and it was never right between him and me. I honestly have no idea why I rubbed him the wrong way, but I did. I attempted to foster a relationship with him by supporting him at different events and even on his birthday, but it did not work.

Once I realized my multiple olive branches were falling on infertile ground, I continued to do so much that I would go to the green room and literally go to sleep while they put my makeup on. It was like putting makeup on a dead body. We celebrated 100 episodes in the first season, which for me was quite an accomplishment considering my work conditions. I don't want to make it seem as if it was all terrible because it wasn't, however, it definitely had its moments and its long days.

The day arrived. It's August 20, 2018. The day started for me just like any other day... Early! I would usually wake up with the stars around 4:30 am to be in the studio at the insanely early time of 5:30 am! My routine was the same. I would wake up, thank God for allowing me to see another day, and then go back to sleep again for the best ten more minutes of sleep in my life! It never fails, I'd fall into a deep sleep and then I'd wake up and jump out of bed like a hooker running out of church. I'd get in the shower and of course shower too long. Now, I am running late. I run out of the house and into the car I go, blazing down the highway.

I pulled up to the studio and the security guard was there as usual. He speaks and I speak; he is very pleasant. He was always so kind and accommodating to me. This day was unlike any other. I zoomed in over the speed bumps, murdering my shocks, and slung my Maserati into the handicapped parking. I have a tag; don't ask me questions and I won't have to lie! As I entered the studio, the sun was rising, and everything seemed normal.

The phrase 'hindsight is 20/20' has never been truer now in my life. I loved being a cast member of Sister Circle Live. My three cast mates were amazing people individually, but oftentimes I felt like I was a cast member of a mean girl movie. It was them against me and it did not go unnoticed by the viewers.

I learned a lot about myself during that time. One of the most important things I learned is that I am stronger than I give myself credit for! If you're anything like me, you too have had to find yourself while being tested. Oftentimes, the test seems impossible to pass. My time on the show taught me I may not have been meant for it, but I am built for it. Being on Sister Circle Live made me feel like everything that I had worked so hard for was NOW finally paying off. I didn't mind the grueling work schedule or even the "I'm on an island alone" feelings. Nor did I care that my cast mates had grown very close like sisters, all while I was treated like a very distant cousin from down south. You know what I'm talking about - we all have one!

I can remember one time finding out that they had all gone to lunch after work and apparently, they taped an episode for Married to Medicine. I had no idea and once I found out, I wasn't fazed initially, but it did hurt after the show aired and many viewers reached out to me wondering where I was. It was clear to me that I was deliberately excluded because we'd oftentimes lunch together after the show was over. So, to not be asked to join them this time smelled like another "Us and not you, moment."

Honestly, that was cool, too. I did what I was supposed to do. I was where I was supposed to be and looked amazing while doing it. I thought it was strange that I didn't really get along with the cast member whom I had the least amount of interaction with. We never really exchanged words but there were a lot of little misunderstandings. Ironically, I thought she was a cool chic. She was fashionable, smart, pretty, confident, and very much into herself. She loved her some her. That didn't bother me much either because I love me some me! I thought she had an amazing body, and her shoe game was always on point. She seemed very interested in who I was, where I came from, and even who my friends were.

When we're both out with our friends, we're often the center of attention and we both take great care of our families. Even sitting next to her for almost two years, I found myself still not really knowing her. I remember when she would always offer to pay for lunch all the time and she would always bring gifts for the other girls, but she never bought me anything. Being a cast member used a different set of muscles. I had to think about how my actions would impact the show, the brand, and even the cast. At first, I was overwhelmed. My life had been turned upside down. I, as a night owl, had to now become an early bird and wake up earlier than I ever had in my life. I had to learn to read from a teleprompter with the critical and judgmental eyes of my stepsisters.

Oftentimes, when I'm reflecting on my experience on Sister Circle LIVE, I often laugh at the fact that they laughed at my confidence and assurance. I honestly believe that they wanted someone they could mold or influence them to be the way they wanted to be. That I could be their puppet and thought that I would be so grateful for the opportunity that I would bend. Despite what they knew, I was well aware of who I was and the light that shined on me. I never once doubted my position on the show or in the world.

The news came that we had the green light for the second season, I was so excited because I knew how hard we worked. It was always our goal to have a positive and entertaining impact on television as black women. Getting awarded a second season was confirmation. We celebrated the second season by popping bottles, eating cake, attending parties, press releases, and everything. I had taken promotional pictures for a second season. I was thinking all along that I was going to be on the show. While taking the photos or getting prepared, my stylist kept asking what color I would be wearing at the photoshoot. No one ever told me what we were wearing. I kept being told by the producer that I could wear whatever color I wanted. That should have been another clue that something fishy was up! I wore a custom-tailored floral red and black suit, designed by my girl Linda Bezuidenhout. All the while the other girls wore yellow, purple, and pink, swearing that none of them knew that my contract was not being renewed. To this day I still find it ironic that they all were color-coordinated for the photoshoot.

I had been speaking with the Executive Producer, EP, about taking off time to shoot a movie for BET. She would never give me a yes or no. I didn't understand why, when everyone else could take time off without question or pushback. On the very last day that I absolutely had to have an answer, she said to me, "Hey, let's go talk" and invited another producer - the second person in charge, to join our conversation.

At this meeting, I was told I would not be going on to the second season. I heard a rumor that they were replacing a host. Of course, this alarmed me due to the fact that I was not like them. I asked the second producer in charge if this rumor was true. The most disappointing part about this is that she lied to my face. She said matter-of-factly, "No, we are not replacing a host." I was so disappointed after realizing she lied to me because I thought we had built a relationship, maybe even a friendship - even down to me attending her son's Bar Mitzvah. She was the one person I thought I could trust the most based on what I thought was our deepening relationship. So, when she was invited to the meeting with me and my EP, I was again very surprised.

My EP and the other producer walked into the room. My EP tried to make small talk, which felt weird and forced. I didn't really understand what I was picking up on, but that was how I felt. She began by saying, "I want to talk to you." The details are sketchy, but the conversation went something like this. My EP began complimenting me on how the fans loved and appreciated me. And even, how she thought that I was a great asset to the show, but unfortunately, she had recently been challenged with increasing the profile of the show. Now, as you know I'm new to tv on this level, so, "increasing the profile of the show," was new to me.

I asked her to explain herself and she did just that. She said, "Kiana, you are great, funny, and amazing. They and we appreciate you. But today is your last day, I'm replacing you with Trina. What would you like for me to tell the press?" It was that cold. I won't lie, I was hurt. I felt betrayed and foolish. All this time I thought our relationship meant more than the ratings. All this time, I considered them as family. We had our issues, but what family does not? Although I didn't like it, I do understand. Trina had one million followers and I did not. And Trina was a Braxton, I was not. So, I guess these considerations made her a higher profile. And I would say, even as sweet and as talented as she is, she never was and never will be "The Kiana Dancie."

I told my executive producer to give me some time to figure out what I wanted her to say to the press. I reminded her that it was my mother's birthday and I wanted to talk to her first. She obliged me with the time and even after speaking with her that evening, she permitted me the opportunity to say goodbye to my fans on live tv, which was very honorable considering that she didn't know what I was going to say or do.

I went home and told my mom that my contract was not being renewed and prepared myself for the next day. I completed the show just like a regular day. No one knew outside of the production team, or so they say, that my contract was not being renewed. I completed the show and was then given the opportunity at the end of the show to say goodbye. It was difficult. I persevered through the moment. Never once was I fully transparent with the viewers about what I really knew. Many assumed I just walked away, not knowing that my contract was not renewed. I never said how I really felt or how many pieces my heart was broken into. I just did what the Dancies have always done - I stood strong and didn't break! However, it was a privilege to say goodbye and tell my family, live on-air, how much I truly appreciated them, and I will forever be grateful for that opportunity and their support.

People ask do I still talk to the sisters. When I see them, I will always speak and wish them the best because I have no ill will towards them. What I have come to fully understand is that God is intentional with my life; all things are always working for my good, (Romans 8:28).

XX - Bye, Bye 2019

Hello 2020, the year of perfect vision. Who would have thought that after having a pajama party for my December birthday, I would live in pajamas for an entire year?! My vision board highlighted all the amazing plans and goals for the year, which included going on tour, finding love, buying an investment property, opening my own business, and even traveling abroad. But apparently, a bat in Wuhan had other plans for me.

We heard there was some sort of viral outbreak in China, but initially, no one was really concerned. After all, we were in America and that just didn't happen here. And word on the street, AKA, Black Twitter, was that Black folks couldn't get COVID19, which at that time was nothing more than a hashtag. I personally love to give all the accolades of truth to Black Twitter, but this one they got wrong. Not only was COVID-19 not just isolated in China, but it also made its world debut in record time.

It hit every continent and every country on the planet, almost at the same time, as if it fell out of the sky. Completely untrue was the thought African Americans couldn't get it, as we experienced the greatest impact for a number of reasons: pre-existing conditions such as diabetes, lifestyle, essential jobs, and social inequalities regarding medical care. Not to mention, some of us didn't believe it was real.

Meanwhile, I was preparing to go on stage with Martin Lawrence during the LIT AF Tour in Savannah, GA, and continue to other cities with the tour! However, God had a different plan. The show was packed with 15,000 people strong. Not a seat in the house was available. Rickey Smiley, DeRay Davis, Bruce Bruce, Benji Brown, myself, and of course, the one and only Martin Lawrence. I was so nervous because this was my first time ever performing with Martin Lawrence. I knew the other comedians on the bill, but he and I never met. I heard he was a gentle and warm soul. Not only was I excited to be there, but I was also extremely humbled.

My stylist had already pulled multiple looks for me, but I knew it had to be a stunner. After looking at the choices, I decided to wear the sequined Tom Ford dress and the Christian Louboutin pumps. With my husband, (gay husband,) in tow, we headed to Savannah. We sang and laughed all the way down and once we arrived at the venue, it was go time!!!! I was greeted by my handler, who took me to do a soundcheck and walk-through. Once I was done, I was shown to my dressing room, with everything on my rider. This included water, food, candies, and a mini-space heater. I'm always cold, don't judge me.

I jumped into my clothes, beat my face, and said the prayer I always say before going on stage:

"Father God, thank You for this gift, this time, and this opportunity. God bless the sound, the lights, and the mic. Let my gift of laughter help mend the broken places in their spirits and in their hearts! Even if it is just for this moment, let them forget about all their troubles and laugh their baggage away."

As soon as I finished my prayer, I got a knock on the door from the stage manager letting me know it was showtime. I was introduced to Savannah like I hadn't ever been before. I had been out with many people including Katt Williams, Earthquake, Kountry Wayne, and Jess Hilarious. Martin Lawrence was always on my bucket list. So, for me, this was a dream come true.

I returned home, not only feeling accomplished but ready for what was to come. I was looking forward to more dates on the road with Martin Lawrence. I had been scheduled to go to Louisiana to meet with them, all to have it quickly canceled by Ms. Rona. I bet you're wondering who is Rona? She is the virus. Rude, disrespectful, and has no concerns about your plans or anything you were trying to do. Ms. Rona split up families and destroyed the lives of babies, grandmas, and Paw-Paws. She's canceled plans, weddings, trips, and even changed the way we buried our dead. Ms. Rona will be one that we will forever speak about.

However, like many, I was able to take advantage of the time we had. I took the time to create a vision board for 2021. I started the *On Live with Kiana Dancie IG Show* and opened my retail business, CPR Cellphone Repair in Duluth, Georgia. I focused on completing the very book you are now reading. I saw Dave Chappelle perform in a COVID bubble. I was cast in a movie titled Christmas Spirit. And, I have multiple shows in development.

Everyone had been speaking about COVID-19, except for the president during that time, who would later confess to downplaying the seriousness of the CORONAVIRUS so as to not cause alarm to Americans. Many people feel that the lack of swift action and intervention by government officials caused many Americans to die. It also led to a nationwide lockdown, which meant no one anywhere could go out of their homes. We were all locked in, trying to slow down the spread of COVID-19. Everyone was scared due to not really knowing how to handle this pandemic and not knowing what to do. We were required to wear masks, wash our hands, (not sure who wasn't washing their hands, but obviously someone wasn't), and maintain six feet of distance from each other.

All of this was very different because most people don't talk to others from six feet away. It was scary, frustrating, and hard. I thought I knew myself before COVID, but being at home 24 hours a day, without the stage, without hanging out with friends, and without anything I considered to be "normal," really made me learn who I was and what was most important to me. This pandemic really tested all facets of my life: my finances, my faith, my relationships, and even my patience.

My growing relationship with Christ severed relationships with people that I thought would be in my life forever. I learned that even when my best friends were not there, God was always there. Not that I didn't know that already, but it was magnified in a way that I feel was needed for this time in my life. I took the time while in quarantine to focus on my goals and strengthen my prayer life. I began to pray Monday-Friday at noon with my church family at Life Changers ATL. It was during these times that God spoke to me in ways like never before. It was honest. It was consistent. It was loving, but sometimes firm. I was grateful for the time that I was able to spend with Him without the hustle and bustle of being on the road. I personally believe that God allowed this pandemic to sit the world down all at one time. How else could you explain it? It didn't matter how large your following was on social media, or how many friends you had. We all were affected in one way or another.

2020 was a year that many referred to as perfect vision and although I was not able to do everything I had on my vision board, it still opened my eyes in a way that I would have never been able to see otherwise. So many people lost their lives to COVID-19. This year will be a year that everyone will talk about for the rest of their lives. From the loss of Kobe Bryant, John Lewis, and Ruth Bader Ginsburg, this year has claimed some of the greatest people on the planet. It was tough for us all.

The virus also magnified the polarization of people when it came to politics, religion, money, and race. Two of the most highly visible victims of police brutality against Black people were George Floyd, who was suffocated with a knee on his neck, and the tragedy that occurred due to the multiple shots and no-knock warrant that killed Breonna Taylor. We all saw Jacob Blake being shot seven times in the back by a police officer in broad daylight in front of multiple people. This caused an uproar and months and months of riots and protests, all due to people being tired of the racial profiling of Black people.

We all struggled, no matter the level we were on. The election of 2020 will be forever marked as historical, as almost 70 million people voted for Trump, and even 10,000 people actually voted for Kanye West. During the election, we campaigned for democrats, high and low. Joe Biden became the 46th

President of the United States. Watching him win this election reminded me to never give up on my goal. Never accept no as the final answer. And no matter your past, it does not have to dictate your future.

If you don't remember anything else in this book, you are the creator of your story. Some of those chapters may have horrible endings. And some may have beautiful beginnings. No matter how it ends or begins, you can always write a new one. Stop looking back at your past wondering what you didn't do or should have done. Set your path on fire and set your future ablaze. Look forward to the things that you want to do - your goals, your plans, your new life. The number one lesson I learned this year is to trust myself, love myself, and be myself. No matter what I go through, God's glory will always be revealed through my life.

I encourage you to make the decision that you won't be held hostage by the baggage of your past anymore. It's time to say, "Bye-Bye Bags, and laugh to lighten your load."

"I consider that the sufferings of this present time are not worthy to be compared with the glory that is to be revealed to me."
- Romans 8:18

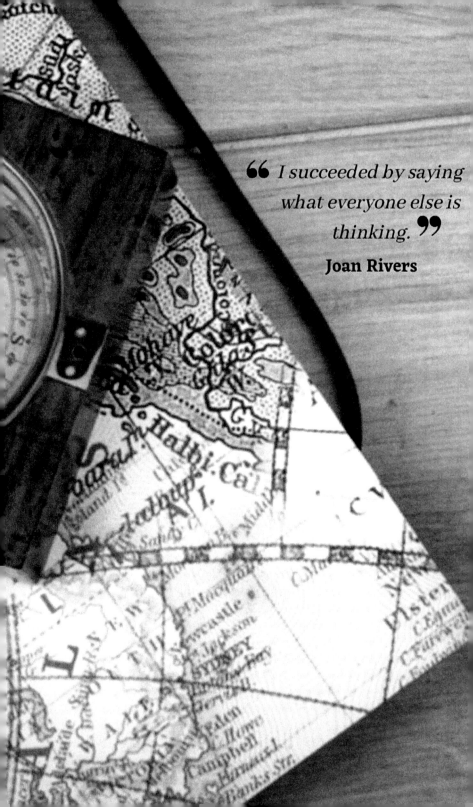

> **❝** *I succeeded by saying what everyone else is thinking.* **❞**
>
> **Joan Rivers**

Checked Bags

LETTERS TO RELEASE EXTRA BAGGAGE

No matter where my life takes me, I think many of us want to find that one moment that feels like a pivotal turning point in our lives. A moment when we leave our past behind and get busy living. We stop making excuses and are ready to do what it takes to have the life we want. The truth is that we are waiting for a moment that may never happen. So, you must make it happen. You can do that through the power of writing. Writing can help you if you've got a lot of emotional

baggage, have a lot of pain and anger, or feel stuck in life. Its benefits have been scientifically proven.

227

It's not only about writing, but more specifically writing letters. It has helped me to get through some challenges and it eliminated regrets that I was carrying. It's not about sending the letters or for the person you are writing to be able to receive the letter and respond. It is a therapeutic way for you to get issues out of your head and put them on paper.

These are letters that I wrote to release baggage I was carrying for too long. They are not letters to tell people off because I didn't get a chance to, but rather to share my feelings, emotions, and regrets. Sharing allows me to feel a sense of release to keep moving forward. However, you cannot heal from what you won't reveal. So, I'll see you at the Baggage Claim!

Letter One

Mommy Dearest,

You are my heartbeat. You make me want to work harder, so you won't have to work at all. I am so grateful for you being who you are. I envy your strength, courage, and compassion. I'm so blessed that you are my mother. I have watched you give everything you have to us. I remember seeing you dog tired, but you still got up every morning to make love sandwiches for breakfast. You were never too tired to make sure my brother, or I, were up and ready for school. Thank you for always picking out my fly outfits and being willing to drive me around. Thank you for still cooking for me and being the common sense when I've decided to do something crazy! Thank you for being my biggest cheerleader! You never gave up on me! I'll admit, I have NO idea who or where I'd be without you. I know you worry about me... I can see in your eyes that you're always praying for me. I want you to know that I will be ok. I'm covered by the blood.

I promise that I will always be there for my brother. I promise when you get older that I will be patient with you. I will take the time needed to listen to you and give you the time to express yourself fully... Even if it takes 10,000 words to say it! LOL! I promise to always dance with you, while we listen to Prince. Mommy, I'm forever grateful for who you are in my life and for your everlasting love and support.

I appreciate you immensely and I love you,

Kiana

Letter Two

Dear Barber A. Palmer,

You have no idea how much you meant to me. I was surrounded by so many loving people and my mom still thought I needed more. So, when she told me she was signing me up for the BIG SISTER AND BIG BROTHER MENTEE PROGRAM, I was surprised but very excited! My memory of you is so clear. You were tall, pretty, kind, and very giving. I remember spending time with you, and it seemed that you got so much out of hanging out with me. I'm sure you had no idea how much your time with me meant. I always felt special with you and was so blessed that my mom, a single woman like you, cared enough to want to see me have the best! I'm grateful for the time we spent together, and I'll forever be looking for you! Thank you for being the best Big Sister I could ever have!

Love,

Kiana

Letter Three

My Dearest Ms. Dotson,

Hearing your voice has never failed to give me joy. When we met over ten years ago, I knew then you'd always be in my life. I remember you telling me, you're a pretty and talented lady, keep pushing and all your dreams will come true. See, what you didn't know then was that I have never met my maternal grandmother and for some reason, you made me feel as if she'd be like you. Spunky, fun, pretty, and doting. You were always, and still are, so supportive and you always knew when to say the right thing to settle my spirit. I have no idea if you even know how much you mean to me, but I wanted you to know there will always be space in my heart for you. I love you for the long talks, the times you came to my shows, the times when we would sip tea and laugh like old hens. I love you for the relationship advice, the quick Facebook notes saying, "Don't stop girl! I'm rooting for you!" and most importantly, the timely prayers. I'm so blessed for having you in my life, and I thank you for everything, although you have NO idea of the impact you've had on my life...

I love you and I appreciate you immensely,

Kiana

Letter Four

Granny,

I remember telling you that you were the best a child could ask for. I know that you did your best, considering the circumstances. I knew, without even asking, the pressure you were under. I knew you wanted to tell me so many things about my father but stayed out of it. Although we never discussed it, I knew you wanted him to do better by his children.

I would call you, and before I could even ask, you would say, "Baby, I haven't seen your Daddy. But how are you?" You knew I was seeking my father to be more present in my life. I never wanted you to carry the burden of his lack of interest or ability, (whichever it was), so that is why I put forth all my energy into fostering a positive relationship with you.

My only regrets are I wish I'd asked more questions. Who was my grandfather? What was he like? How did he die? Where was he from? Where did you meet him? Who are you? Really, who are you? Not just my grandmother and my father's mother, but what's your favorite color? How many siblings did you have?

What about Granddaddy? Now since you, Granddaddy, and my father are gone, those are questions that may never be answered. I'm writing you this letter to simply say thank you.

Thank you for loving me in ways my father didn't know how to.

I love you,

Kiana

Letter Five

Granddaddy or Daah,

As we so affectionately called you... I miss you. I miss your big, strong hands holding mine. I miss playing with your thumb that got cut off from jumping trains! I miss looking into your big eyes and listening to your crazy stories!

I miss your scruffy beard and your beautiful brown skin. I miss your gap-toothed smile. Although I miss yours, you gave me my own. I miss your voice. It was rich with a great tone. I miss your laugh. I worry that one day I'll forget your smell as the years pass by.

When growing up, it was never a thought of mine that you'd not be here to see me as a grown woman or see me get married. I remember sitting in your lap, and while you held me with one hand, you drank coffee, black with a little sugar. I was so spoiled, they said you carried me around till I was seven years old, simply because I didn't want to scuff the bottom of my shoes.

You always made sure that I had a few dollars in my purse that I carried. I will never allow the joy in my heart for you to go away. You were the best grandfather I could ever ask for.

I wish you were here, still living, laughing, and yes, telling us stories about your train-hopping adventures. I love you and will always miss you...

XOXO,

Yana

Letter Six

Grandmother,

I imagine that if I had ever met you, I would probably call you granny. I don't know, but what I do know is I have always dreamed about you. I wish I had grown up with you versus growing up hearing about you. Hearing how amazing, kind, and pretty you were always warmed my heart and made me smile. Hearing how great of a cook you were and how you'd let my mother comb your hair after you came home from work reminded me that you probably would have allowed me these same privileges. I was told so many stories about you, like, how great you smelled considering Chanel No. 5 was your favorite perfume and how you were known to wear a fur stole even though you rode the bus back and forth to work.

Granny, I think about you every day. There's never a day that I'm not wondering what life would be like if you hadn't died when mommy was nine. I'll tell you, being born on your birthday has made me feel especially close to you and even more excited about sharing that day with you. My mom, your youngest daughter always said, she knew I would be born on that day. It came to her in a dream, and she never questioned it. It was said I was a gift from you to her and in her opinion, the best gift she's ever received in her life. I am blessed and very honored to be your grandbaby, the only one who shares your birthday. I pray that I have always made you proud! I love you immensely...

Your birthday twin,

Yana

Letter Seven

Eric,

I'm only calling you by your first name because you are no longer the fat baby you used to be. When mommy first told me she was pregnant, I was literally numb. It had been just the two of us for fourteen years, and nowhere on my radar did I see you or any sibling, to be honest! I've always prayed for her to meet a good man and he would eventually marry her, but never did I think she would have a baby!

Anyway, she did have a baby, and let me tell you, it was like I had one too. We were inseparable from day one! When we went into the hospital to deliver you, they wouldn't let me come in, and I was a nervous wreck. I was scared, I was happy, I was anxious but more importantly, I was excited. You were coming and although I never wanted a sibling, I embraced the fact that I was about to become a big sister and I vowed to be the best!

Eric, I fell in love with you on the first day I met you. You were the most beautiful, perfect thing mommy could have ever given me. I loved you from that day as if you were my own baby. People would always say that you may as well have been my baby. Although you were not my child, I made a promise to myself and even you, that I would do my best to protect you. I would do whatever I could to make sure you were great! Whatever you needed, I would make sure you had it! This is a promise that I have never broken.

Now, look at you, handsome, independent, and God- fearing! I know that I haven't told you in a while, but I am very proud of the young man that you have become. No matter what you have been through or have encountered, you have never given up! Although it didn't surprise me, I'm fully aware that everyone has a breaking point, but you have never let it come to that! You have been through it all and you've bent, but never have you been broken. I give you the utmost respect and I salute you. Over the years I have said many things to you but always remember this, "You are enough ... You have been given ALL the tools you'll ever need to be great! It's within you. Never doubt your greatness, (it's natural to do so), but when and if you are not sure

PUSH!!! Pray until something happens!" I love you dearly…

Your big sister,

Yana

My Little Brother & Me

The Kiana Dancie

Letter Eight –
To My Future

Hunnie,

That's the name I'm imagining you would answer to when I am calling for you to kill a spider or help me with some other task that I could clearly do but would prefer not to especially since I have a whole husband. I'm writing this letter without even knowing your name, where you are from, how you make a living, or even your favorite meal or color. I just want you to know that I pray for you every day and I dream about our life together. It seems kind of cheesy, but I've planned our wedding too. Some days, I see our wedding as a huge event with lots of friends and family, but then other days I see that we've run away to a far exotic destination, and we return in marital bliss! Either way, it's just me and you! Our way. Our story.

I've questioned why it's taking you so long to find me, what you are doing and who has your attention, while you are not my husband. I look forward to late movie nights and random bae-cations.

I look forward to cooking for you and holding your hand while walking through the airport or just stargazing. I look forward to having deep conversations with friends over food and drinks in our beautiful backyard and to becoming the mother of your children. I promise to be your peace in times of war. I'll be your joy and your safe haven. I look forward to growing old together. I look forward to praying together. I want to say thank you for being the man I waited for but mostly being the man I prayed for... I love you...

Your future...

Kiana

Epilogue

T he moral of the story is that all baggage isn't bad. The key is that I had to know the difference between baggage that would weigh me down and cause me to miss my blessings versus the baggage that's similar to the fear I needed to ensure I didn't burn my hand on the stove as a kid. I learned that some of the baggage I was carrying was there to save me, guide me, and remind me of the past to ensure I did not repeat it.

My role, in essence, is to manage my bags. A process that takes constant practice to master. I continue to identify the things that have no value right now, and the things that will hamper my journey now and in the future. Just because they are of no use to me now, does not mean they will never be of use. I would never take fur to Hawaii, so the bag that carries the fur stays home until the season is right. On the other hand, if I am headed to the beach, I want the bags with the shorts and swimsuits.

As long as my bags are packed right, I'll be ok. Keeping baggage from the past will leave no room for happiness in the future. Enjoy life by limiting your emotional baggage to a small carry-on. The worst part of being strong is no one ever asks if you are ok. Find balance, be vulnerable to a degree while being strong, and carry your bags proudly, tossing what you no longer need. When people question your motives or why you do what you do, tell them to walk a mile in your shoes, see what you see, hear what you hear, and feel what you feel. Maybe then they will understand why you do what you do. 'Till then, don't judge, and mind your own bags.

"He will once again fill your mouth with laughter and your lips with shouts of joy."
Job 8:21

The Kiana Dancie

REFLECTION QUESTIONS

Whew, chile!

That was a lot to take in, huh? Hopefully, this book is helping you to release your own baggage so that you can live your best life! I use this book as a healing process and I hope you, too, will find ways to heal and release your own baggage. I pray that you find pieces of you in the stories I've shared that you could not only relate to, but that you can reflect and learn from to address, deal with, and release any unwelcome baggage you are carrying.

Take some time to answer the reflection questions on the next page.

- What are some of the bags you have carried and why?

- Who, besides yourself, do you feel is responsible for these bags?

- Have you candidly discussed the pain and effects that are associated with that baggage?

- What steps have you taken to unpack your baggage?

- How have you, or are you, healing from your baggage?

- How are you setting your past on fire and setting your future ablaze?

- How will you help someone else to say Bye, Bye Bags?

Baggage Removal:

I challenge you to remove the baggage from your life... I want you to do the following:

Write down 1 thing that reminds you of a:

1. FAILURE
2. INSECURITY
3. SHORT COMING

Then ... TEAR IT UP AND BURN IT!!!

Decide to NEVER be held captive or hostage by any of these things again!!

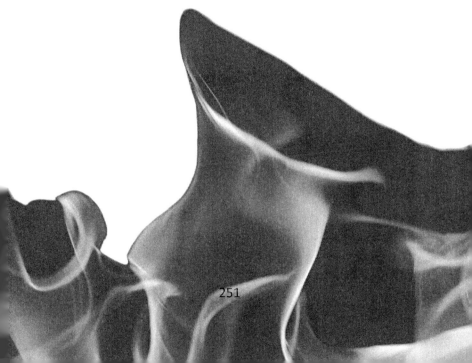

RESOURCES TO ASSIST

My humor touches on some very sensitive subjects at times, but all in a way to make someone smile through their pain. In light of that, I have provided a list of resources should you or a loved one need assistance.

Alcoholics Anonymous 24-Hour Hotline:
1-856-486-4444
www.aa.org

Al-Anon/Alateen:
1-800-344-2666
www.al-anon.org

Alzheimer's Association Hotline:
1-800-272-3900,
www.alz.org/we_can_help_24_7_helpline.asp

American Psychiatric Association:
1-800-847-3802
psychiatry.org/patients-families

National Domestic Violence 24-Hour Hotline:
1-800-799-7233
www.thehotline.org

National Eating Disorders 24-Hour Hotline:
1-800-931-2237
www.nationaleatingdisorders.org

National Suicide Prevention Lifeline (24/7):
1-800-273-8255
suicidepreventionlifeline.org

Sex Addicts Anonymous 24/7 Hotline:
1-800-477-8191
www.saa-recovery.org

Substance Abuse and Mental Health Services
Administration (24/7):
1-800-662-4357
www.samhsa.org

BE A FIRESTARTER

Join me and other women like yourself who have the desire to become happy, whole, and healed! My circle of sisters, also known as FIRE STARTERS, refuses to spend another day being mad or sad about the past! We have decided to set our past on fire and our future ablaze!!! Join the Facebook Community and let's start a fire!!

~The Kiana Dancie (Yana)

YOU ARE NOT THE BAGS YOU CARRY!!

The Kiana Dancie